He made his prediction ☞ W9-AWU-739
long before any scientists knew there were holes
in the ozone layer. Yet Edgar Cayce foresaw this
and other developments in his many visions.
Now a new generation is discovering the wisdom
and foresight of Cayce, and how it can guide us
through the next century.

IN THE NEXT MILLENNIUM . . .

✧ We will communicate with each other without
the use of technological devices, but through
the power of our minds.

✧ Society will learn to get beyond the stultifying
divisions of race and skin color, to create a
new age of social justice.

✧ People will communicate with life on planets
outside our solar system.

✧ Oil will become obsolete as a fuel, and the
ocean will offer up its riches.

EDGAR CAYCE
ON THE MILLENNIUM

EDGAR CAYCE
ON THE MILLENNIUM

EDGAR CAYCE
ON THE MILLENNIUM

JESS STEARN

WARNER BOOKS

A Time Warner Company

WARNER BOOKS EDITION

Cover photo by Michael Agliolo/Stock Imagery

Warner Books, Inc.
1271 Avenue of the Americas
New York, NY 10020

Visit our Web site at
http://warnerbooks.com

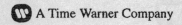 A Time Warner Company

Printed in the United States of America

First Printing: August, 1998

10 9 8 7 6 5 4 3 2 1

A Preface

The prophets of doom and gloom are at it again. If El Niño and the sun spots don't get you, it will be the shift of the polar axis. Well, the polar axis has shifted before, and our precious earth is still spinning around the sun at a dazzling speed. So what if it should hit the sun or get so close that we're toasted on one side and roasted on the other side? Gravitation. Of course, gravitation. The law of gravitation constraining the planets from colliding. And where did that come from? Obviously, the same source that rules our planet, our solar system, a greater solar system just discovered for the Millennium, and all the other solar systems waiting to be discovered by our vigilant scientists. Doesn't it ever occur to any of the doomsayers that the same Universal Mind that pervades the planets has a hand in keeping us from falling off our spinning earth, likewise has control of something like a polar shift? And will keep us from predicted icy or watery graves—if we remember to thank Him for our being here at all. Yes, there is a God, the God of the Universal Mind and Divine Law, with whom the Ancient Prophets and Jesus Christ spoke and were spoken to.

As Edgar Cayce knew so well, all of life is a testing ground as well as a learning process. For every dark cloud there is a bright light of hope that we keep alive with our faith in a Lord who didn't give us life without hope. His greatest gifts, as Cayce noted, were that of love and free will. Free will by our actions and beliefs, our love for the parent earth and all that is in it, to curb the turmoil in the bowels of the earth and the tides of the sea. And also keep us happily spinning around our sun at a breathtaking speed without falling off into space because of the way the Lord crafted His universe.

Cayce
A Prologue

Edgar Cayce got to the core of life and living as no man since Jesus Christ. He told us what we were doing here on Planet Earth and why. Though he foresaw the future and clarified the past, he was more than a prophet or soothsayer. More than a healer of illness, for he showed the sick how and why they were sick and how they could heal themselves with help from an abundant and bountiful nature. He taught us that we were children of the Universe and that we belonged here in this life as we had in the past and would again in the future.

He saw each person as a unit of energy on the earth, a creation of the Universal Force we call God, an entity distinct from every other being on the face of the globe, who deserved to be treated as such. Thus his suggestions and recommendations were invariably different for each seeker who came for help in body, mind and spirit—for the material as well as the spiritual.

He saw each man, woman and child as an eternal being born into the earth plane for a purpose. And he pointed the way to the realization of that purpose. He sought not only wellness but wholeness for the multitudes who presented their problems to him—though more often than not he tuned in to a variety of these human problems from a piece of paper with only a name and address on it. He could tell at any designated hour if that person had left that particular place—whether it was home, a ship or a hotel. He was asked to give a health reading for a habitually inebriated screen director whiling away time in a game of bridge with three colleagues at the Savoy Hotel in London. In the midst of saying the director should be temperate in his habits, Cayce observed in a subconscious state back in his Virginia Beach study, "What a wonderful hand." The people monitoring his reading were puzzled. But in London the director and his partner had notched a rare grand slam—a perfect hand in bridge.

Cayce's mind could obviously travel through time and space at will to disperse information that led to innumerable cures and revelations. In his altered state of consciousness his subconscious tuned in to a Universal Intelligence that was like some vast computer network, supporting if not clarifying Einstein's postulation that there was no time or space in the real world. And his mind was the creator. In his sleeplike trance Cayce could place any cell in the body and tell why it was hurting, and what had to be done to ease the hurt, invoking remedies in nature for virtually every kind of disease, which, he said, was nothing more than disease. He could look into the future on both a personal and grand scale. More than sixty years ago he foresaw a tilting of the earth's axis that would bring a global warming of the earth only now being noted by environmentalists. A warming that he said will have considerable impact without the cataclysmic consequences predicted by the prophets of doom and gloom. He saw traces of an Atlantean civilization on the floor of the Atlantic Ocean near the Bahamas, where undersea explorations turned up fragments of man-made paving stones and marble columns washed over by the ocean for thousands of years. He peered psychically into the tombs and vaults of the ancient Egyptian pyramids and the Sphinx, referring to the lost records of an Atlantean incursion. And, incredibly, he saw the return of many Atlanteans by the Millennium. Only recently archeologists confirmed his descriptions of the Egyptian structures and their secret chambers. Long before they were found, he described the precise location of the Dead Sea Scrolls in Israel and described the contents and the biblical role of the Essenes with remarkable accuracy. Information of earthshaking importance would flow out of him in response to the most trivial questions. A businessman, squeezed by World War II, inquired in 1941 when his business condition would improve. Cayce replied in four years—August 1945— when the war would conclude with the defeat of the

Japanese. He foresaw Hitler's rise and subsequent sur-
render—the month and year—at a time when the German dictator's armies sat astride all of Europe but the
British Isles. He picked out a time frame—1958 to
1998, the eve of the Millennium—for the beginning of
great eruptions in the bowels of the earth reflecting the
human turmoil on its surface. He pinpointed the great
Alaska quake in 1964 and more recent quakes in San
Francisco and Los Angeles—both cities not fully re-
covered and both apprehensive about a recurrence before the year 2000. He saw the rebirth of religion in
agnostic Soviet Russia at a time when the churches
were closed and Christianity was banned. And the
deaths of Franklin Roosevelt and John Kennedy in office, though he, Cayce, had passed on in 1945, fifteen
years before Kennedy's election. Thirty years before
they occurred, he foresaw the race riots that swept the
country and which he said would be ongoing until the
American people made an extra effort to care for each
other.

Pragmatically, as he saw how accurately his psychic
observations defined the past and the present, he came
to believe in an endless cycle of life. Though he could
consciously grieve for those who knew sorrow and
pain in this lifetime, he felt there was a lesson to be
learned that would be helpful the next time around.
"Death is a beginning," he said, "a passing in and a
passing out." Not unlike the seasons and their changes.

He so often said as an axiom of life, "You get to
heaven on the arm of the person you're helping."

Cayce did not have an easy time in a world where he

made life so much easier for so many people. From childhood in western Kentucky, a farmer's son, he was thought strange and shunned. A neighboring priest crossed the street when he approached Cayce's house. Others laughed at him openly. He endured it all with the resignation of the biblical Job. He was only four years old when he showed the first signs of being the man he was to become. He had been sitting on a horse with his Confederate-veteran grandfather when the horse, terrified by a bear, reared up and trampled its rider. The grandfather covered the boy with his body. At daybreak a searching party, including the boy's parents and neighboring farmers, came to the scene. The boy's father, Leslie Cayce, knelt and saw that his own father was dead. He turned to his wife, Carrie. "My pa's dead," he said. "He died saving the boy."

The boy rubbed his eyes and said, "He's not dead, Pa. He's been talking to me. He says he's all right." Edgar's father winced in embarrassment, while the neighbors looked at each other and shrugged.

As he grew up he had visions of angels, particularly a Lady in White, who spoke to him when he was distressed. He dismissed these as idle dreams. He was slow in school, seeing visions of a mystical Atlantis, while younger classmates were learning about Columbus. He had no friends. He would go to his grandfather's grave for comfort and sit against a tree and nod off with an open Bible in his lap. As he dozed he saw as in a dream the Lady in White, who said he would do great things one day. "Do not despair. You will find your way. For the Lord makes wise the simple and enlightens his eyes." Only that morning the teacher had consigned him to a classroom corner to don a dunce cap. He had stood up and, with a dignity uncommon in one so young, walked out of the class. That night, on the staircase, he overheard his father saying, "He's made us the town laughingstock. He couldn't even spell *cabin* in school today. He's impossible. He sees things that aren't there, and hears voices nobody else does."

Tears came to his eyes as he knelt that night to say his prayers. Through the mist of the tears the Lady in White reappeared. "What shall I do?" he asked the misty figure. "Sleep on the spelling book tonight and you will be able to spell every word," she replied. He put the primer under his pillow that night.

That morning, at breakfast, his father put him to a test. He not only spelled every word correctly, but he knew the page the words were on. The father tossed the spelling book away, thinking it a trick of some kind, while Edgar's mother hugged the twelve-year-old boy and said, "Listen to your own heart. And never doubt the Lord."

The boy smiled. "It's not the Lord I doubt, Ma."

Chapter One
The Great New
Planet Earth

"**W**here is the safest place to live?" a minister concerned about the approaching Millennium asked Edgar Cayce.

"Don't worry so much where you live but how you live." The Sage of Virginia Beach replied, "Make the family of man your family as well."

It was an answer he gave the many. For his farseeing psychic mind told him that when man raised his consciousness and mended his ways, loving his neighbor as he loved himself, the destruction he saw was not inevitable. Cayce had visualized the devastation of a power-drunk and greedy Atlantis, broken up in remnants in one day, and had feared the same would be visited on the great cities of this nation—the modern

Atlantis—if it did not open its heart to the downtrodden and oppressed.

"The Lord," he said, "marks the fall of the smallest sparrow. He knows how so many in authority treat the infirm and the aged. Look at the Napoleons, Caesars and the like. Rather than casting themselves in God's image they made Gods of themselves. And were destroyed."

There would be some destruction: Earthquakes and volcanoes, violent ocean storms and global warming, predicted by Cayce decades ago, with shifts in the polar axis and powerful bursts of solar winds whipping into our atmosphere from various directions at a dazzling velocity of more than twenty thousand miles a minute, bringing on the El Niño tidal waves and other climactic changes.

He warned of the Vanishing Shield—the ozone layer—in the earth's magnetic field, diminishing the protection from the damaging solar rays. He foresaw a Death Ray, a by-product of laser research in America, with which ancient man eliminated the dinosaurs on Atlantis and our primitive earth. He predicted the Death Ray would turn up on the earth in some twenty-five years, and so it did, put together by scientists at the University of California laboratory at Berkeley. It has not been activated.

He saw dramatic extensions of human life, with centenarians commonplace, along with cures for Alzheimer's, cancer and other malignant diseases of the aging. He visualized the genetic birth of new life, long before cloning became a popular word.

Optimistically, modifying predictions of worldwide disasters, Cayce saw a rising consciousness in man, as the biblical end of times moved into the new Millennium marking the dawning of a New Age, exalted by the presence of "the One who had come before with the promise of everlasting life. And would be a light unto a new generation already affected by an increasing spirituality as though the Christ influence was already here."

He saw a burst of new ideas in communication, as though the secrets of Atlantis' advanced technologies, buried under the shifting ocean sands, had evolved out of minds that remembered that distant past.

"There will be new sources of energy, supplanting the poisonous gases from automobiles, trains and smokestacks that annually pollute the air with endless tons of the toxic gases, carbon dioxide and nitrous oxide. Water, broken down into its component parts, hydrogen and oxygen, then electrified, will become the principal energy source. Light and heat will be drawn from the sun's rays, warming huge buildings and private homes in cities wholly sustained by their own power. Plagues [AIDS] will be eliminated but not until tens of millions of lives have been lost around the world. There will be massive desalinization of Atlantic and Pacific coastal waters, bringing an end to droughts and famines on this continent. And new discoveries of other solar systems and new life."

Like the prophets of old, Cayce was concerned not only by what we humans thought of God but by what He thought about us—and considered that His com-

mandments could no longer be ignored before a righteous retribution by cataclysmic strokes of nature. In-
equities in the social order, said the fundamentalist
Cayce, were trying the Lord's patience. But redemp-
tion, though overdue, was still possible.

"There must be greater consideration of each individual, each soul being his brother's keeper. There will
then come about political and economical relationships where there will be a leveling in society.

"For as the period draws near for the changes that
come with the new order, it behooves idealistic individuals and groups to practice what they preach.
'Though the heavens and the earth pass away, my word
will not pass away.' And that word was, 'Love thy
neighbor as thyself.'"

Cayce's critics smiled, but the Virginia Beach soothsayer only sighed and renewed his warning.

"Unless His word of brotherhood is considered there
must eventually come a revolution in this country and
wars between brothers. For these are the leveling
means to which men resort when there is plenty in
some areas and a lack in others. Crime, riots and every
form of disturbance arise when those in authority do
not consider every phase of human activity and experience."

Despite many prophecies of doom and gloom by
scientists as the Millennium neared, the long-term
future looked bright to Cayce. The main thrust of the
Four Horsemen of the Apocalypse—war, death, pesti-
lence and famine—will be met by a convocation of nations establishing a permanent armed confederacy to

keep the peace, lest a nuclear holocaust wipe out civilization as we know it.

"Whatever man has done he can undo. Man is not ruled by the world, the earth, the environs about it," said Cayce, "nor the planetary influences with their associations and activities. Rather man brings order out of chaos by his compliance with Divine Law. By his disregard of the Law of Divine influence, man brings chaos and destructive forces into his experience. For a less chaotic world, live by the Ten Commandments, with its love thy neighbor as thyself, and the Sermon on the Mount.

"Great upheavals in the earth may be brought about by violations of the Divine Law. Only then shall the forces of destruction take over within the bowels of the earth as they have in the minds of men in wars that have taken millions of lives—born and unborn—and left great cities and nations in ruin."

Cayce was optimistic, while deploring the dissension in organized religion as a blot on man's conscience. "More wars, more blood have been shed over racial and religious differences than anything else. But these differences will be soon mended."

I couldn't help but think of this years later as nearly a million Americans of every race and color, and Christians of every denomination, including Jews for Jesus, participated in a religious love fest at the nation's capital on the eve of the Millennium. Blacks and whites from all over the country were trading handshakes and hugs as they praised the Lord. Cayce had foreseen it all in a promising era of benevolence and brotherhood. The end of the apocalyptic time, times and a half of the Bible and the beginning of a new mind-opening age with the advent of Christ. Cayce, toward the end of his life, spoke of Christ's presence as though it was already a reality in bettering man's relations with the Lord.

"With the advent of the Son of Man on the earth, giving man an advocate with the Father, there will be an influence to counteract much of the retribution from misuse of the authority given governing the laws of the Universe.

"As for the precise time. No one knows, even as he gave. Only the Father."

Until then it would be a testing period, with God's children on probation in their little playpen.

Cayce saw the course of events with a telescopic eye. Back in the 1930s he saw improbable Allies join to beat back the anti-Christ emblematic of an improbable Axis coalition of Germany, Japan, and Italy. Thus preserving the global peace for the century.

He was ridiculed when he saw Communist Russia as the hub of this alliance, but he persevered. "Atheistic Russia, freeing itself from the shackles of Communist tyranny, will become the hope of the world," the Sleeping Prophet announced to the chagrin of his own followers.

Somewhat shaken himself, he gave additional readings which saw the democratizing of the Soviet Union, with the liberation of several Soviet states, and a friendship with the "great enemy" America, saying a miracle from the skies would occur before this event took place.

Nothing seemed more improbable at this time, when Stalin's Russia loomed as a global menace, not until a nuclear accident rocked the town of Chernobyl in the Russian Ukraine on April 26, 1986. The physical impact was great. But the spiritual and emotional jolt was even greater, with millions of people affected by the nuclear fallout that swept across the skies of Soviet Union and Northern Europe.

There were dark whispers among the tens of millions of Russian peasants that the tragedy was the Lord's retribution against a Godless nation that had forsaken its ancient faith. Rumors that it was all in the Bible spread like wildfire through the land. Bibles were scarce in atheistic Russia. But a black market in the Holy Bible soon flourished behind the Iron Curtain. "It is all in Revelation, God's promise of things to come," the peasants cried, as they smuggled Bibles into their homes. And sure enough, it was. For the English word for *Chernobyl* was "Wormwood." And it was wormwood that presaged the evil to come in the destruction and fire spawned by God's wrath. An ominous passage in the prophetic Book of Revelation sent a shiver through a population already terrified by the fallout casting a pall over Europe:

"And there fell a great star from heaven, burning as it were a lamp, and it fell upon a third part of the rivers, and upon the fountains of water.

"And the name of the star was Wormwood.

And many men died of the waters because they were bitter."

The Russians asked themselves what it meant that a third part of man would be killed by fire and smoke, and by brimstone. They could visualize another Hiroshima, where the afflicted would pray for a death mercifully ending their agony and misery.

"And in those days shall not find it. And shall desire to die, and death shall flee from them."

It got no better as they combed through the Bible. The prophet Jeremiah castigating leaders "who walk in lies and strengthen the hands of the evil doers, as in the days of Sodom and Gomorrah. [Jehovah] will feed them with Wormwood and make them drink of the water of gall."

Just as he foresaw the Christianizing of Russia, Cayce saw the most populous country on earth, China, gradually turning to Christ, prior to any swarming of missionaries over the land. The spirit came from within the country itself, as though the hand of God had touched them and said, "Listen to the wind."

There were signs that appeared to support Cayce's belief in a rising consciousness. Small things, perhaps, but nevertheless bellwethers of sweeping change. A golf game. Not that much in the tide of human affairs. But significant, as television replays showed an elite white gallery at a Georgia country club cheering on a youthful Tiger Woods over all-white rivals as he went on to win a prestigious Masters Tournament on a southern course where he wouldn't have been allowed a few years earlier.

No less significant was Tiger Woods' acknowledgment of that victory on television when he was asked about blazing a trail for black people.

"I am not black," he said in a statement that bothered some and inspired others. "Nor white, yellow or brown. But a member of the human race."

As Cayce said so often, it was all in man's hands—in this instance the hands of twenty-one-year-old Tiger Woods, with his benign outlook, along with his golfing skills.

"One man or ten with their hearts graced by the Lord can make a difference," said Cayce. "For it is not the world, the earth, the environs about it, nor even the planetary influences that rule man."

Geologists and seismologists were not as optimistic as Cayce. The Big One in California—bigger than the quake that demolished San Francisco in 1906—is yet to come, they say. "The question is not whether a giant earthquake is coming," said Dallas Peck of the U.S. Geological Survey, "but when and where."

Wherever there has been a major earthquake, the geologists say, there will likely be another. California, rocked again by a frightening quake in the San Francisco area in 1989, can expect quakes of even greater magnitude within ten or fifteen years. The entire Mississippi Valley is threatened. The most likely area for the biggest Big One is the basin of New Madrid, Missouri, south of St. Louis, where in 1811–1812 a series of quakes was powerful enough to rock twenty states and reverse the flow of the Mississippi.

"Tension has been building ever since in the New Madrid area—and it could erupt at any time," geologist Dallas Peck has warned. "A catastrophe such as the one that killed ten thousand in Iran recently, and eight-hundred-thousand in China, is inevitable, even in a fault-ridden Manhattan, amid all the skyscrapers reaching proudly into the sky."

Not unlike Cayce, a Cal Tech seismologist was aware of the natural forces that are working slowly but inexorably under the earth, out of sight, unnoticed, setting off reactions and counterreactions in fragile earth faults deep in the bowels of the earth. There was no reliable way, despite all the scientific research, to predict them—except for the behavior patterns of animals trying to escape the doomed area. Nobody but the horses, dogs, birds, fish, rats and cockroaches, fleeing their forest or city homes, seem to know with certainty when a temblor is about to strike, and then, alas, only a few hours before the event.

In Yellowstone National Park in Wyoming, the day before a major quake the forest became silent, and visitors wondered at the absence of the chirping birds. They didn't wonder long. Twenty-four hours later a devastating life-threatening quake shook the wild nature preserve, uprooting trees and buildings and causing widespread damage. Showing some primal connection between animal life—closer to nature than man—and the natural forces brimming under the surface of the earth. And in its heavens.

Edgar Cayce saw the sun, the center of our solar system, as God's gift of life. "The sun, as ruler, has a direct effect on the inhabitants of the earth as well as its plants and minerals. The sun reflects those inner turmoils, with its sun spots and solar winds that stir people's emotions, earthquakes, and wars around the world.

"The sun spots are but a natural consequence of that turmoil inside man which with love for the Lord predisposes him to a sunny nature. Know that the mind is the builder. A spot, a blot, on the life-giving sun or a burst of radiant light given unto those who dwell in darkness and cry aloud to the Lord for courage and hope."

Courage and hope—qualities that were Edgar Cayce's during his rocky journey through life. Early on he was mocked and laughed at by scientists and educators who never studied his gift. "Impossible," they said. "No man can do what he claims. Healing people without seeing them, prescribing remedies that no self-respecting doctor would even know about."

He was not even dismissed as a quack. He was a freak. The elderly dean of the Virginia Beach medical fraternity, Robert Woodhouse, approached by a delegation of younger physicians, was asked to bring charges of practicing medicine without a license against Cayce.

He laughed. "You fellows don't get it. This man isn't practicing medicine. He comes to me—and my wife goes to him."

Cayce was in a sphere all his own. He was able to

simplify the immensity of a boundless heaven where a sun thousands of times the size of our earth was in turn dwarfed by a star in another solar system thousands of times larger than our sun.

"As a child of God's Universe, cast in God's image, man should be aware," Cayce said, "of life-giving interchange of cosmic rays between the planets, notably the sun, and the earth with its spark of human life." The great scientists—Einstein, Copernicus and Galileo—divinely inspired like Cayce, were very much like him, affirming our connection to God's infinite world.

"The more you become aware of your relationship to the Universe," Cayce said on many occasions, "the greater your ability to apply the God-force within you, and still greater your responsibility toward your fellow. For as you do to the least of men you do to a sun which reflects the turmoils in man, stirring up earthquakes and wars."

He asked listeners to look into themselves and not think of the sun as the ruler of the earth, but of the Lord as the ruler of the sun and as mindful of its welfare as He is of man's. For one could not exist without the other.

"If you wish the ruler of the earth—the sun—to hearken to the voice of that power which created it, and gave it light, you should realize that the solar body with its sun spots so often reflects the discord in your life and your responsibility to your fellow man. For as you do unto others so you do unto your God."

The changes Cayce saw in the earth seem to have

taken on a new vibration—not surprising, since the earth and its sister planets never stay still. They are always moving and with movement there is always change. Cayce said we should look on these celestial bodies as our friends, for they keep us in touch with our Universe. We must think positive. And where earthquakes are concerned, keep from expecting the Big One of the doom-and-gloomers momentarily. "It doesn't have to happen," said Cayce. "Just keep the earth's slate clear, so God doesn't have to wipe it clean."

Cayce's predictions weren't so much about earthquakes. Where some saw a disaster, he saw a new world born, with the bright promise of a dawning Aquarian Age. Which rests on God's gift of free will— the only one of His creatures so blessed.

"Our experiences are changeable, open to choice, as we let the Creator come into our sphere," said Cayce. "As we get to know our earth better, with all its ups and downs, men will come to the realization we are all part of the same family and have a collective destiny. So we may as well enjoy it. Peering into a far better world than we have known before."

Chapter Two
The Second Coming

Jesus of Galilee was Edgar Cayce's companion. Cayce thought of Him as his Guide. For one who turned daily to the Bible, this was a very personal connection. Jesus came to Cayce in both his waking and sleeping hours: sometimes in visions and often in dreams. As a boy, so much by himself, Cayce saw Jesus in His robe and sandals, treading through narrow streets, the sick holding out their hands in supplication. He saw Jesus reach out and touch a leper as the motley crowd shuddered. And all cried out in wonder as the afflicted man stooped and kissed the hem of Jesus' robe and sobbed, "I have felt the hand of God."

As a boy, Cayce never mentioned any of this to anyone. It seemed so natural to him. For the Bible moved graphically through his mind and Jesus seemed like an old friend. He walked with Him as He trod the sacred ground of Jerusalem with His apostles. It was not surprising that Jesus would appear to him in the approaching Millennium, more often than not in the quiet hours of the night when Cayce slipped into the dream state. One dream was so special, so sharply defined, that Cayce as a young man shared it with friends who had gathered around, knowing from the look in Cayce's eyes that he had something unusual to impart.

They listened avidly as he spoke of his dream. It had come unbidden, and it had held him enthralled. His friends were struck by the glow on his usually placid face. It was a dream he would always remember. As would his listeners.

"It was three o'clock in the morning," he said. "I could see the hands of the clock in my dream. A man came to me, someone I had never seen before, and said, 'Do you want to go to a meeting?'

"I said, 'I don't know. I don't go out very much.'

"This person then said to me, 'This is a very unusual meeting. I think you will enjoy it.'

"I asked, 'Who is going to be there?'

" 'The Master is going to speak.'

"We went to the meeting. It was in the most beautiful place I have ever seen. We entered a long hallway. The light was a dark blue, opalescent, and made our flesh look purple. As I looked around I realized that all of the people there had passed over. No one was there in the flesh except myself. There was a man with a halo about him I took for Jesus. I didn't know the person who had asked me to come. Those around me were mostly preachers, the Reverend Dwight Moody, an evangelist, and others I could not name.

"There was a light. I couldn't see it, but realized in the odd way of dreams that it came from an unseen Voice. There were no benches or chairs. Everyone was standing. Dressed in robes. It was the Lord speaking. He was not visible.

" 'Who will go to bring peace to the earth?'

"Jesus, who had been standing near me, stepped forward and said: 'I will go. It is time for me to go again onto the earth, though there will come forth from our friend here [referring to me] a messenger that will proclaim my day.'

" 'When and where?' the dreamer asked. The Voice—the Lord—replied, 'In the hearts and minds of those who set themselves up to be a channel in the purpose and desires of that physical body. As has been given of old [in the Bible] the sun will be darkened and the earth shall be broken up in many places. And then shall He be proclaimed through the spiritual interception in the hearts and minds and souls of those who have sought His way, His star will appear and will point the way for them to enter into the holy of holies within themselves.' "

The time was not clear to some and Cayce elaborated:

"There will be the upheavals in the Arctic and the Antarctic that will make for the eruption of volcanoes in the torrid areas and there will be shifting then of the poles. So that where there has been those of a frigid or the semitropical will become the more tropical, and moss and fern will grow. And these will begin in 1998, heralded as the time when His light will be seen again in the clouds. As to seasons, as to places, it is given to those who have named the name, and who bear the mark of His calling and His election in their bodies. To them shall it be given."

Cayce was speaking of the few chosen by the Lord to mark Christ's resurrection in the new Millennium.

They had listened entranced. "Please explain," said one, "what is meant by He will walk and talk with men of every clime?"

Cayce replied, eyeing each person.

"As given, for a thousand years with men everywhere, then in groups, in masses, and then the first resurrection in a thousand years. When the changes will come.

"In the searching out of those who, where, and when He speaks, or has spoken among. By their fruits you shall know them. They that bring more righteousness—the children of faith, hope and charity. Those of the spirit, a channel that may walk with Him. Let not your heart be troubled. Neither let it be afraid. Giving self to seeking day by day to know the will of the Father as manifest in Him. And may be manifest in you. For He will not leave you but will come to you. But only if invited. As when He walked with men as the Master among men."

There were still some puzzled frowns.

"Always with the will of the Father, He walked and talked with men in the various stages of development through the ages. Even as Joseph in the land of Egypt, when those of that land were giving counsel to many nations."

Another hand went up. "How will we know him?"

"Perfected in body, overshadowing the ordinary figure of man, He will make himself known. Just as the various developments of man through the ages have been noted at those times when He walked and talked with men without their feeling any more than His presence."

He paused and looked around. There was the ghost of a smile on his lips. "He tarries not and the time draws near."

He had returned before in spirit, in times of crisis, infusing His will at the peace conference in Geneva, at the end of World War I, into the heart and soul and veins of one not considered an unusually Godly man, President Woodrow Wilson. Yet Wilson was raised to be a channel for the world.

And so was born a League of Nations, the gift of the Christ, Cayce was saying, though its leaders, as Cayce saw, were not dedicated enough to maintain the peace when the league was swept up by World War II.

A strict fundamentalist, Cayce was baffled when he gave his first reading concerning reincarnation. He was appalled as the reading was read back to him. But as he fell back on his Bible, he read about the apostles asking Christ whether he had been the prophet Elijah in a past life. Christ replied that it was not He but John the Baptist. There were other biblical references of reincarnation by Christ, such as, "Before Abraham was I am."

"How," they asked, "could he precede Abraham, when He was no more than thirty years on the planet?"

But gradually, going over what Jesus said, reincarnation seemed to make sense. In his lifetime Cayce had met many people he felt he had known before, liking some at sight, others raising the hackles on the back of his neck. He remembered the places and events that checked out. His saving the life of a young boy on a riverboat who later jumped up into Cayce's lap as he recalled the experience.

He could visualize treading the streets of the Old City with the Savior and his followers and how thrilled he had been. Was it his imagination? Yet even if imagination, it had to come out of something. Was this why as a boy he had clung to the Bible, not skipping through it as some did, but burying his nose in a book whose pages had become ragged with use? He had particularly liked the red ink, not only because it was the word of Christ, but because it represented the blood He had given for God and mankind.

He recalled the apostles asking Jesus whether a blind man He had helped had been born blind because he or his parents had sinned, indicating they were thinking in terms of a previous life and its karma. Jesus had replied, "That the works of God might be made manifest in him." The question implying reincarnation more than the response.

It was obvious to Cayce, or anyone who could read, that the disciples believed in reincarnation. Which did not necessarily make it so but did give some indication of the belief system of the early Christians.

Who, thought Cayce, could be more Christian than the disciples or the Master?

Consequently, he breathed easier whenever his readings got into past lives. "If it was good enough for Jesus and His twelve Apostles," he told Gertrude, his wife and aide, "it's good enough for me."

He told friends on another occasion that they were witnessing a new Dawn. With a worldwide need for a reassuring message from Jesus at a time when Cayce foresaw missiles weighted with atomic bombs traveling with the speed of thought to any objective.

"In His Millennium there was a looking forward to the coming of the Messiah. Today there is an expectation of the Prince of Peace. As He was sent before and will be gladly received again. By those who know Him by this light.

"You have already seen Him in spirit," Cayce said of the Second Coming. He sat still for hours, his hands folded, waiting for the Christ spirit to visit him. It seemed for a moment almost as though he could reach out and touch Him. He remembered something said about helping Jesus to warn the people. Was this his purpose in life? Or was he just deceiving himself out of vanity and ego, two faults that march together, each feeding on the other?

No, he could not deceive himself. For then he would be deceiving others and be false to Christ, he thought. The words spilled out of him. His voice, usually gentle, vibrated across the room. Unconsciously, he slipped into biblical cadence. "You have seen His spirit in the leaders of all realms of activity, in the aisles of the sea, the wilderness, the mountains, in the activities of every race. For what must be obliterated? Hate, prejudice, selfishness, backbiting, unkindness, anger, passion and those things of the mire, slime that are created in the activities of man.

"Is He coming today in the earth? Yes, in those who cry unto Him from every corner. For He is the Son of light, of God, and He comes again in the hearts and souls and minds of those who seek to know His ways. This is hard to understand by those mired in the flesh, where avarice and vice holds sway. Yet those who call on Him will not go empty-handed. For He is the spirit of God, and His messenger."

The hands went up.

"Will he return with His disciples? With Peter who rejected Him, or Judas who betrayed Him for thirty pieces of silver?"

Cayce, almost in sorrow, shook his head. "What did He stand for? Forgiveness and love. He later embraced Peter and what did Peter do? He founded a church in Christ's name."

And Judas—the arch-scoundrel of history?

"He is to be pitied. There was no one more prophetic than the Master. How else could He have done what He did? When He tossed the sop across the table at the Last Supper and it stopped at Judas's place, He already knew what His trial was to be, and as He told John the beloved, He went to the Cross with the love of the Father to show that life was everlasting.

" 'For this my Father loves me, because I lay down my life that I may take it again. No one takes it from me, but I lay it down of my own accord. I have power to lay it down, and I have power to take it again.' "

Cayce's eyes traveled around the room. He could see that some were confused.

"You wonder how you will know when He returns. That answer lies within you. For He is not only the light to the flock that follow Him but to those everywhere in need. His promise has ever been. 'If you will open thy heart, thy mind, I will enter. And abide with thee.' "

The day of miracles was not past. For Cayce was proof of that. There were few in the group now listening to him whom he had not healed in mind, body, and soul. He knew how much depended on their faith, already weakened by misfortune or illness.

He urged his listeners to visualize their dreams. "With these dreams of the Master," he confided, "has come a strength, when I feared I had not the will to go on, I'm still a bit dazed each time the assurance comes and fearful—like so many blessed by His presence and have turned the good, this strength, into self-serving purposes.

"When that remembered Voice again asked, 'Who will warn my people,' I boldly volunteered. Then out of a throng came the Master, Jesus. He blessed me and said, 'I will go with you all the way.' "

Cayce smiled. "I was ready then." Even giving a dozen readings during a day when his own readings told him he should do no more than two for his own

health's sake. But with his two sons overseas in a
bloody war, he could not deny others whose pain he
felt.

While his dreams often seemed unreal and self-
delusionary, they gave him the hope he needed to summon the strength to help himself and others:

"I regretted that I didn't have this depth earlier. It
gave me new assurance that God is mindful of the
children of men, responsive to their prayers, directly or
through Christ. In a world of uncertainties our only
link to the Lord was our vision of Christ."

As before, Jesus was to have his forerunner, said
Cayce. John the Beloved of Christ, who always sat by
His side. "There is soon to come into the world a body
that to many has been representative of a sect, a
thought, of a philosophy, yet one beloved of all men in
all places where the university of God in the Earth has
been proclaimed. There the oneness of the Father is
known and is magnified in the activities of individuals
who will proclaim the rising day of the Lord. Hence
that one John, the Beloved in the Earth. His name shall
again be John.

"You ask where and when is to be His one? In the
hearts and minds of those that have set themselves in
that position that they become channel through which
spiritual, mental and material things become one in the
purpose and desire of that physical body. Beginning
the New Age of spiritual awakening. As to the spiritual
changes that are to be as an omen, as a sign to those
that this is shortly to come to pass, as has been given
of old, [Matthew] the sun will be darkened and the

earth shall be broken up in many places. And then shall be proclaimed through the spiritual interception in the hearts, minds and souls of those who have sought His way, that His star has appeared and will point the way for those who enter into the holy of holies in themselves."

As Cayce aged and his connection to the earth became tenuous, his dreams about the Master were more frequent. In one dream, as heartwarming as any he experienced, he appeared to have been invited to an evangelical meeting by two ministers whom he had met but once. They took him to a large revival meeting. The tent was crowded, and the air teemed with expectation. There was a large screen that took up one side of the tent, and flashes of lightning in the distant background. Through the open flaps in the tent, Cayce could make out a great white cloud that seemed to dominate the heavens.

He asked one of the ministers what the meeting was about.

The minister looked at him in surprise. "You don't know?"

Cayce shook his head.

"The Lord our God is about to speak to us."

At this point a Voice, clear and strong, resonated out of the cloud and lightning, saying, "Who will warn my children?"

As if in response, the Master emerged from out of the throng, clad in a simple robe and sandals, saying in a strong voice, "I will warn my brethren."

The Lord then spoke in a voice that made the tent

tremble, addressing the Master. "No, not now. The time is not yet fulfilled for you to return to the place you were. So who shall warn my children?"

One of the ministers spoke up. "Why not send Cayce? He is here now, and ready."

The Master nodded. "Father, Cayce will warn my brethren."

There was a vast silence, and then a thunderous chorus of eager voices from the assembly. "And we will help Cayce," came the cry.

Cayce could see the smile on the Master's face. And the dream closed down. He was puzzled and concerned, troubled. How could he live up to his dream?

Chapter Three
Money for the
Millennium

He made more millionaires than the runaway stock market of the 1990s. And he was more versatile. "Clients" came to him for all manner of financial advice, making their fortunes in real estate, business ventures, the stock market and the racetrack. And yet he lived and died poor because he wouldn't use his psychic powers to make money for himself.

He saw nothing wrong about people making money with his readings, as long as they did it for others. Supporting the family, getting a son or daughter an education, buying a home, or giving to the less fortunate. He was big on homes since he was a long time acquiring one, thinking that he would lose his gift if he misused it to help himself.

He saw the country becoming the world's financial center by the Millennium and his only fear was that the quest for money would exceed the search for God.

"Sooner or later we will understand that the biblical story of our Creator was no fable. For God as we will see one day is Creation itself. This takes in every planet in our solar system, and other systems. He listens to the smallest voice. He is a Universal Spirit that Jesus fathomed, and where He gained his strength, the strength to live and to die, to ultimately show life was everlasting."

Cayce didn't negate the value of money, only the love of it. Jesus drove the moneychangers out of the temple because their greed was an offense to the Lord. He deplored the gulf between the rich and the poor, and preached that things had to be evened up. And this will come with the increased Christ consciousness of the Millennium.

Cayce lived penuriously most of his life, when he could easily have been independently wealthy. Those close to him had the feeling that he felt an affinity for Jesus, who never owned more than a robe and a pair of sandals.

No one resisted great wealth more cheerfully. When he turned down a Hollywood offer of a half million dollars to check out their scripts, he told a studio boss, "I'm not that big a star."

"I couldn't believe he'd turn it down," the film mogul said, "when he was doing so many readings that helped people get rich, without charging them a dime."

What he didn't realize was that Cayce, with his special vision, was doing what he could to instill a love of his fellow man into others that would forestall the global problems he had foreseen with the Millennium. Feeling as he did that the violence erupting under the earth was a reflection of the hostility and greed on the surface.

He saw hard times, and he saw good times. He knew when it was time to invest, and time to keep your money in the bank or under a pillow. The advice he gave, moneywise, was invariably in response to questions about a certain stock, business or property. He often wondered whether he had been drawn to Virginia Beach, Virginia, then a sleepy little resort, from Selma, Alabama, because of a premonition that the real estate boom was coming in the beach city and he could help friends profit from it.

Cayce downplayed his influence on the real estate market:

"People are certainly going wild on Virginia Beach property. I don't know whether it's because we came here from Selma, Alabama, or whether we came down from Selma because of what it was going to be. According to a reading we gave on real estate this afternoon, property here is going to advance the next few years from fifty to a thousand percent. So if you invested a thousand dollars, the best price would be a million dollars. Unbelievable but true. There will be many new millionaires, the prices constantly increasing. I can only hope they spend their Millennium money wisely and think of the next man."

As Cayce saw, the residential values to the north of

Laskin Road were worth four or five times those to the south.

An NBC reporter, impressed with Cayce's predictions of the city's growth, dubbed him "this marvelous man who had knowledge possessed by no other human being."

He pointed out that Cayce didn't go to Virginia Beach until the latter part of his life—going there because one of his readings said that's where he should settle. When he decided to move, he knew nothing about the town and had never seen it. The name had come to him out of the blue—like his predictions. He and his family were disappointed to see the sleepy little fishing village near Norfolk. But since other people followed his readings, Cayce thought he should, too, and there he settled. Soon he began to make friends. One of these friends was Russell Hatchett, then City Manager of Virginia Beach. To him and many others, Cayce made his predictions of the tiny town's astounding growth. Nobody believed it at first, because the town was building south, and Cayce said it would be moving north.

The City Manager looked at him in disbelief. Later, as the land development process reversed itself, he reversed his opinion of Cayce. "I was amazed with Cayce's vision regarding the values in this area. That he should have been able to hit the turnabout, with its spectacular rise in values. Property to the north end has advanced in price some ten times what it was at the time that Cayce made this prediction."

And this some thirty-five years ago. The prices have

been soaring ever since. It didn't hurt any that the East Coast's largest naval base was at neighboring Norfolk, the port embracing a wider area known as Hampton Roads.

Cayce had predicted, "Within the next thirty years, Norfolk with its environs is to be the chief port on the East Coast, not excepting Philadelphia or New York."

Cayce sensed the indecision of some prospective homeowners. Because of his confidence in the city's growth he urged many to make their buys before the property got away from them. The prices were rising so fast that even a month's delay might be costly.

"Respecting the acquiring of a home as indicated you will find there is a twenty-five to fifty percent advance already in the properties, whether it be a farm or a home that might have aided in preparing the way for a good life. The sooner the decision the better. And do prepare, wherever it may be, so if it comes to the worst you can sit down and grow something to eat. You won't be hungry if you are wise and make preparations."

Though he didn't speculate in local real estate and become a millionaire like so many of his devotees, Cayce did manage to buy a pleasant house to the south. Prices there were so much cheaper that even he could afford a place with a garden of beautiful flowers that he talked to, and a small pond to the rear of the house. He invited a houseguest, a friend of his son Hugh Lynn, but warned if he didn't come early he wouldn't recognize the neighborhood:

"Most of the little frame buildings along Seventeenth Street have been torn away or are being torn away. They are being replaced with brick, and we're putting on the air of a real city. And the dwellings— goodness! You can't look anywhere without seeing new places going up."

He had seen the whole Virginia Tidewater area prospering, including the cities of Norfolk, Newport News, Hampton and Portsmouth.

He saw this age of the Millennium as very special because of his expectations of Christ's presence—emphasizing the presence and not the person. He foretold that Jesus would make Himself known in His own way, echoing the biblical references in the New Testament. Believing in reincarnation, Cayce expected to be around for the occasion in one form or another.

Virginia Beach had no more than twenty thousand people when Cayce arrived with his wife and two small children. People came to him with every imaginable problem as his reputation spread. They inquired about their health, about business, the stock market and jobs. Some looked at him doubtfully when he suggested they buy homes to the north, when the town was so obviously building up to the south. Nobody knowing the construction of a bay-tunnel bridge to the north would eventually transform the modest little resort into the largest city in Virginia with almost a half million people. A Millennial event Cayce had foreseen.

"When Virginia Beach had no more than thirty thousand people," a Cayce friend related, "he told me to buy a couple of properties for five thousand dollars. I asked why he didn't buy it if it was going up fifty times or more as he said. He laughed kind of wryly and said he couldn't do it even if he had the money, as profiting from what he did would diminish what he was trying to do. Which was helping others, not himself. He was strong on this brotherhood business, saying people had to think of their fellow man more or they'd stir up all the adverse elements like earthquakes and volcanoes and tidal storms. It sounded a little far-fetched to me. But I gave it a little more credibility when land values soared in the areas he specified as if there was no ceiling to them. It took a few years, but I held on, and eventually the land was worth five hundred thousand dollars. Land was going up like this all over the place, always to the north.

"I wanted to do something for Cayce but he wouldn't take anything from me. Only the twenty dollars he got for a reading. And if people didn't have the money, that was all right, too."

A few years after Cayce had settled in the beach city, he wrote: "To think that the readings told me years ago that this was the place to move to. Had I invested five hundred dollars in real estate here—from the profits today on that five hundred dollars I would have been able to fulfill my dream of building a library and teaching center with the two hundred thousand dollars I would have had. However, it will come in time if the good Lord wishes."

And it did, eventually, along with a hospital, from the donations of grateful millionaires for Cayce's nonprofit projects.

Even after Cayce had passed on, he was making

millions for people who followed his readings and took a plunge in property he had recommended.

He was very high on the city in Virginia that his Universal Mind had led him to. Without elaborating, he often said it was the safest city on the East Coast. He was the local real estate man's best friend. Asked while in trance about the future of Virginia Beach, he replied: "This, as we find, would require a great deal of speculation on the part of individuals. As we would find, and as we give, of all the resorts that are on the East Coast, Virginia Beach will be the first and the longest lasting of the increasing of the population, valuation and activities. Hence, the future is good."

I saw how the boom worked myself, long after Cayce's passing, when friends asked me to join them in acquiring a two-hundred-acre tract plumb in the area where Cayce's readings said prices would burgeon. I could have easily obtained a $28,000 bank loan for the one-third interest in the property. They were well-meaning friends: John Smith, a pioneer builder of Virginia Beach hotels and an early supporter of Cayce, and John's wife, Virginia. They took me over the wooded land in an impressive tour. While I admired the landscape and saw its possibilities, my interests were in California where I lived.

But John and Virginia were old friends. So I said, "If you need the money to close the deal I will gladly come in with you."

They smiled and shook their heads. "No, we just thought that Cayce would like you to profit with us from wherever he's marking time. You forget, you wrote *The Sleeping Prophet,* the book that gave him new life."

I gave them a quizzical look. "So you think he's still around."

"Oh, yes, he'll be back for the Millennium."

A few years later John passed on. I attended his services and spent some time with Virginia in her bereavement. Eventually she settled the estate. The property had not been mentioned in the intervening years. I had forgotten it completely.

Virginia looked strained. She had just come from her lawyer's. She sighed as she looked at me across the luncheon table.

"How I miss John." There was a mist in her eyes. "I never had to think about any business. John was so efficient. And he loved Edgar Cayce so."

The name had come out of nowhere. Suddenly her face brightened. "Do you remember the property John wanted to share with you?"

I thought a moment. "Vaguely."

She had an impish look. "You'll never guess what it's worth today."

I was very aware of the spiral of prices for residential land in Virginia Beach.

"I hope you get a good price."

She hesitated a moment, as though she wished she hadn't said anything.

"You can get it out," I said. "I know what's happening."

She made a little face. "All right. Your twenty-eight

thousand would now be worth two and a half million dollars."

I was not surprised. Everybody in Virginia Beach who knew about Cayce was getting rich but Cayce— and me, it seemed.

I reached for Virginia's hand. She was a dear friend. "All I can say is I'm glad you got it."

And I was.

I wouldn't have known what to do with all that money. Journalists and writers of books were seldom millionaires. Unless they listened to Cayce.

Laskin Road in downtown Virginia Beach became one of the principal shopping and business centers. But the developer, Jacob Laskin, unfortunately for him, knew nothing of Edgar Cayce or his predictions, and probably wouldn't have listened had he heard. For Virginia Beach was a close-minded city then, happy about its small and neighborly context, and indifferent to "outsiders."

Years after the Laskins left the street that was named for them, Gladys Davis, Cayce's secretary and aide, met Jacob Laskin's son while visiting in California. When she told him about the explosive growth of the street they had built, he said rather ruefully, "I guess we should have held out longer." They might have, had they known there was an Edgar Cayce who was on top of the real estate market, like he was just about everything else.

Cayce was a wonder with anything financial. Wall Street brokers heard of his penchant for picking winners and prodded him for information on stocks, promising him a bonanza. He rejected the offers, but later met a businessman interested in financing the hospital Cayce dreamed of, staffed with friendly doctors and nurses. With a hospital for the sick and disabled as a goal, Cayce had no qualms about making money.

"I can see," he told his wife Gertrude, "where the ends may justify the means." He wouldn't be doing it for himself but for others. Gertrude wasn't so sure. But she, too, thought of all the good that could come of it.

Wall Street was booming. You could punch a pin through the stock tables and come up a winner. Everything was going up, even as cracks were quietly beginning to appear in the economy. Soon with the rising market there was enough money to build the hospital on the Edgar Cayce foundation grounds overlooking the Atlantic Ocean. Cayce's dream had come true.

The year was 1929, and Cayce's readings showed a growing concern with the economy. He began to advise his benefactors to withdraw gradually from the market, contenting themselves with the profits already given them. As the Fall neared, his advice on getting out of the market grew more urgent. But the speculators had amassed a fortune so easily that they thought it was no time to get off the gravy train. Cayce warned that a break was coming on Wall Street that would affect the whole country. There would be a panic in Wall Street and the banks would close. The economy would be paralyzed. But the speculators weren't intimidated. Cayce had to be wrong this time. Greed won out, and the speculators lost a fortune. The hospital was closed, and Cayce's dream was shattered. Typically, he blamed himself. It was the last time he participated in any project where he would be a beneficiary. Nor would he knowingly give a reading for the object of making money. However, the forces of greed were everywhere—including his own family, where his father, a failure as a farmer and a storekeeper, lulled Edgar into a secret relationship with a Yankee doctor, Wesley Ketchum. The sole object, ostensibly, was to heal the sick unable to find help with more conventional medicine. Cayce felt comfortable with the relationship in the beginning. He would make the diagnosis in his sleep, suggest a remedy, and Ketchum would oversee the convalescence or perform whatever surgery that was required.

In time, as his gift was misused for financial reasons, Cayce, as he had been warned by his wife, suffered severe headaches, feeling dazed and shaken. He had no recall of what he was being asked in the unconscious state. Meanwhile, as the "incurably" ill began to get well, Ketchum, previously ostracized by Southerners still fighting the Civil War, prospered, as did Cayce's father, who had masterminded the partnership. Ketchum justified his deception with the comforting assurance that he was saving lives in the process. Cayce's father said the same, and he lost his son's confidence.

The partnership remained pretty much a mystery until Hugh Lynn Cayce, the mystic's son and new head of the Foundation after his father's death, looked up Ketchum's wife in a small town near Los Angeles. He asked me to join him and we visited the ninety-eight-year-old Mrs. Ketchum together. She was sharp and alert and her eyes brightened whenever she mentioned her husband's name.

"Were you aware," Hugh Lynn asked, "that your husband gambled on the horse races from tips given him by Edgar Cayce in his sleep?"

The bright eyes twinkled. "All I know," she said with a smile, "was that my husband had the biggest racing stable in the state of Kentucky."

Chapter Four
The Pole Shift—
and More

The Profits (correct) of doom and gloom, the alarmists, are at it again. The world they see—or profess to see—is heading in a collision course to extinction. When that old polar axis goes into its dance, Siberia is going to become India, and India is going to wind up in South Africa, and South America and the United States may have a merger. Or something like that. It has all happened before (then what are we doing here) and it will happen again—almost any day now, though no one is sure of the exact time. And Cayce is saying quite the opposite.

We have El Niño and global warming, and they've already arrived, so we don't have to speculate what they're going to do to us. They've already been busy

off the coast of our neighbor to the south—Mexico—
in Acapulco, Indonesia and California, and that's
something we can understand and sympathize with,
and see how we will deal with it ourselves, in as practical a way as we know how. But glacial ice packs,
three-hundred-mile-an-hour winds, and huge mastodons
and mammoths turned into oil deposits by floods that
swept mountains away? That's something else again.
What can we do about all this but examine what Edgar
Cayce has to say about our prospects? He's visualized
a lot of hell and damnation before, earthquakes to blast
cities off the map and tides that will overwhelm the
flatlands of various countries. So he's not the prophet
(correct) to hold back when people are sitting on the
edge of their chairs with all those scientists and psychics salivating over the destruction they see with their
dark glasses.

Cayce had a number of things to say about pole
shifts. He was asked about them by scores of concerned people—some of them scientists—way back in
1939, namely about a pole shift he had predicted.

"Will it [the shift] cause a sudden convolution and
about what year?"

The Sleeping Prophet replied in his sleep: "In 1998
we may find a great deal of the activities as have been
wrought by the *gradual* changes that are coming about
during this change between the Piscean and the Aquarian Age. This is a gradual, not a cataclysmic activity in
the experience of the earth in this period."

Five years earlier, Cayce was a little more explicit in
a reading that caught my attention because of devas-

tating volcanic eruptions on the island of Montserrat in the torrid Caribbean Sea. Eruptions predicted by him in oblique fashion:

"As to the physical changes there will be upheavals in the Arctic and the Antarctic that will make for eruptions of volcanoes in the Torrid areas, and there will then be the shifting of the pole—so that where there has been those of a frigid or the semi-tropical will become the more tropical, and moss and fern will grow. And these will begin in those periods '58 to '98 when His light will be seen in the clouds."

Late in 1997, as I write this, global warming, believed to be caused by sun spots, caused by a polar shift, was being blamed for bringing about droughts drying up masses of land in the torrid zones around the world.

Cayce had put a start on the polar shift, which others had speculated about. But he did not see it as catastrophic or cataclysmic, as many geologists and other self-styled experts did. In a five-year lapse between two readings mentioning polar shifts there had been a number of earthquakes and sizable storms around the world but nothing of a catastrophic nature.

What Cayce saw in 1939 he saw again for the Millennium's dawning. He was asked what great change or beginning of change, if any, was to take place in the earth in the year 2000 to 2001.

He replied simply. "When there is a shifting of the poles. Or a new spiritual cycle begins."

He saw the shift in stages. Without any reason for alarm.

A humanist above everything else, Cayce was aware that the "turning of the axis," as he put it, had an effect on the earth's magnetic field, which with the active sun spots affected the climate in varying degrees. But his emphasis on gradual changes from a shifting pole was a clear indication that he didn't anticipate any catastrophic surprises. There were no warnings, with which he often couched his dire predictions, only a suggestion for man to mend his ways and live by the word of the Lord.

Comparing this country with Atlantis, he mentioned a vastly different pole shift for someone with an incarnation in that distant civilization, relating to its storied past. Speaking of the Atlanteans' problems with eighty-ton dinosaurs overrunning the country, he touched on the plans to exterminate the monstrous beasts with a Death Ray when the people got help elsewhere—from a natural source that appeared to be heaven-sent: A polar shift exterminating the animals before the Atlanteans could use any nuclear force.

"The entity [the subject listening spellbound] was then among those who were gathered to rid the earth of the enormous animals which overran the earth, by shifting masses of ice, nature-God moved the poles in such a way that the animals were destroyed."

To Cayce, the entity was not only the physical presence of a person but his spiritual essence carried over from a previous life that Cayce was now outlining. The man listening, according to Cayce, had been an Atlantean in a past existence. And his subconscious mind revived at this time memories of Ages and places long forgotten. Memorable for him, but just another incident in the life of America's greatest seer.

It was characteristic of Cayce that he brought God into the situation, sanctifying the massacre of the huge animals without a clue of how human life was spared in what must have been an earthshaking incident.

What Cayce sensed in his sleep, the leading seismologists and astronomers have been losing sleep over. A Cal Tech seismologist noted plausibly, "The natural forces that shape our destinies are working slowly but inexorably under the earth, out of sight, unnoticed, setting off reactions and counter-reactions in fragile earth faults deep in the bowels of the earth. We have no way of knowing when the next quake will strike."

Cayce talked of the 1998 shift in the earth's axis, ushering in the Aquarian Age, which may precipitate modest changes in the earth's climate. Scientists agree that changes may have already been caused by the resulting weakening of the magnetic field that shields the earth from solar winds and cosmic rays, already raising worldwide temperatures and reducing the ozone layer, which protects us from an excess of ultraviolet rays. Skin cancer is on the rise, with more than one-fourth of the adult population in the U.S. Sun Belt affected and downunder Australia restricting its beaches in the summer months.

Dr. Keith McDonald, a research physicist at the U.S. Department of Commerce, involuntarily supported Cayce's predictions, saying that the slippage of the earth's axis engendered enough heat to gradually affect the protective magnetic field and its ozone layer.

Cayce maintained a positive attitude, saying that with the earth changes there comes a corresponding challenge in people's lives, making them aware of the God who holds their lives in His hands. Without the Lord, life at best is tenuous. Yet with all the hardships that accompany the natural changes wrought by the shifting of the poles—the quakes, the hurricanes and the ocean tides—an optimistic Cayce assures us that humanity will recover from its climatic trials and tribulations with a new consciousness of its connection to its Maker.

"He will not give us more than we can endure," Cayce stressed. "Whatever comes, as we look into our deepest self, He will give us the strength to work toward a brave new world that begins with us. For we cannot say often enough that just as we handle our daily lives, as we treat our fellow man, so shall we create the elements in nature that bring serenity out of turmoil, and peace out of war. Man may forget but God remembers. Not to punish, but to live in His image as He has said. It is all up to us equally. For no man is greater than another in the Lord's eyes."

As the shifting of the axis goes on, we can all be heartened, knowing it is a prelude to a bright new world. The dawn of a more creative age. The Aquarian Age. Man entering into a partnership with the Universe, using the energy from the sun and other planets—notably Jupiter, with its cosmic rays—to clear the atmosphere, just as it clears his head of negativity and teaches that forgiving is for-giving. As the Lord forgives.

Again and again Cayce stressed we can stand up to whatever comes, which he accented will not be that difficult. We will find we have a new friend in Mother Earth, knowing that what we do affects the earth just as the earth puts demands on us:

"Whether the hearts and minds of individuals or souls [given authority concerning the laws of the universe] are fired with the thoughts of dire consequences or rather a spiritual awakening, then there is an awareness of that which is in the making in the affairs of the nation and the universe. In relation to Mother Earth."

Cayce saw life as a testing ground, with the Lord fixing the playing field and making the rules, yet ready to help if man responded to His first commandment, whatever the conditions: "Thou shalt love the Lord thy God with all thine heart, and thy neighbor as thyself."

Many were impatient with Cayce's piety at a time when they were pressed to keep their lives together, not realizing, as Cayce knew so well, that what was inside a person ruled what was outside, whether it was an earthquake, flood or fire, or a Depression and the absence of love.

"So live each day, each hour, in the spirit of truth and faith in the Lord, so as to practice those influences in your own life and the life of all you contact. For the Lord has said, 'Though you wander far afield, if you will cry unto me, if you will ask, if you will draw nigh unto you. My arm is not short as man's counting of shortness, but will bring to you that which is the desire of your heart, if conceived in righteousness.' "

Ironically, while the scientific community viewed Cayce and his "witchcraft" with tolerant smiles, plain common sense brought many scientists unwittingly into his camp.

"The climate reality is that if you look out your window, part of what you see in terms of weather is produced by ourselves," noted Thomas Karl, the lead scientist at the National Climatic Data Center in Asheville, North Carolina. "If you look out the window fifty years from now, we're going to be responsible for more of it."

Karl blames this part of the warming globe on a world fueled by greenhouse gases—principally carbon dioxide, produced by the burning of coal, oil and natural gas.

Unlike Cayce, Karl doesn't get into the cause of this aberration: man's greed. In some areas like California's coastal waters, the temperature in 1997 was five degrees warmer than in 1990. And increasing.

"You have to go back millions of years to find global temperatures like that," Dr. Thomas Crowley, a paleontologist-climatologist, told the *New York Times*.

Crowley painted a darker picture than Cayce. Sea levels rising a foot and a half, flooding low-lying coastlines, while droughts devastate the torrid part of the world, Africa and Central America, as the agriculture in the Northern Hemisphere prospered because of the heavy rains.

There were other changes, attributed to pole slippage, seen by Cayce and detailed in his readings and conversations: "The magnetic field which shields the earth from solar and cosmic radiation had been weakened to the extent that it has become a vanishing shield, posing an increasing threat of mutations of plant and animal life and widespread climatic changes, contributing to global warming and malignant skin problems."

Cayce attributed the increased radiation to the uneasy axis moving gradually from its ice-pack position. His assessment was supported by some scientists, with no thought, as Cayce had, that the human spirit could turn things around.

When the increased radiation became apparent, Dr. Keith McDonald postulated that a concentration of heat from the solid inner core of the earth increased fluid activity near the polar regions, slowly destroying the magnetic field. He saw a long period without an effective shield against excessive radiation. And then, as had happened in the past, for some inexplicable reason the process would be reversed. Cayce would have said it was explicable—a benevolent God at work.

In the last three hundred years, McDonald says, the magnetic field, with its ozone layer, has decreased some fifteen percent, with corresponding larger amounts of solar radiation reaching the earth's surface as disturbances occur on the great gaseous ball of light around which our planet revolves. "When this radiation reaches the earth atmosphere, it is trapped by the magnetic field which arches high over the earth. These areas, the Van Allen belts, stand as a shield between the sun and earth, protecting plant and animal life from excess radiation."

There may be a reversed series of climatic changes during the next few years. Lush valleys becoming barren wastes, deserts blooming, ice caps covering the land, polar caps melting, flooding the southeastern United States and other low-lying coastal areas of the world. Blue-eyed, fair-skinned people may have to stay indoors to shield themselves from the sun—either that or wear long-brimmed baseball caps and dark glasses that come down to the ends of their noses.

Edgar Cayce took a different view. "It could all be turned around," he told Gladys Davis, his lifelong secretary, who jotted down every one of his readings. "All we have to do is respect the Lord."

"He saw the best in every earth change he foreshadowed," she said, "and would concentrate, meditating with Christ and the Lord to hold back the solar winds and rays bombarding the earth."

Cayce short-circuited the scientists by his ability to tune in to the Universal Intelligence, yet he did go over many of the explosive readings he gave, comparing them to what the scientists said about what he had to say, not troubling himself with their research into ancient records and paleontology.

In not seeing a long-term ozone problem, Cayce differed from the scientific mainstream, which saw the ozone hole or layer widening with the continuing pole slippage and the widespread use of chlorine pollutants. Meanwhile, New Zealand's Institute of Water and Atmospheric Research reported the ozone hole in the magnetic field over the Antarctic covered an incredible ten million square miles of the stratosphere, affecting Australia as well.

The ozone layer's thickness, the scientists reported from satellite data, was at near record lows, with sixty percent less ozone than some fifteen years ago.

Meanwhile, major newspapers in America, alarming their millions of readers, while seeking to reassure them, were rolling out editorials urging the federal government to act promptly to protect the ozone layer in the North American stratosphere. The U.S. Environmental Protection Agency, already alerted by the National Aeronautics and Space Administration, responded immediately in the decade ushering in the Millennium.

As NASA saw, the damage to the ozone layer was twice earlier estimates. Again it was clear that thoughtless, greedy men in industry had self-inflicted with unbridled use of chlorofluoro-carbons in solvents, air-conditioning, and refrigerators. It never occurred to anyone that the chlorine gas used to kill hundreds of thousands of men in devastating wars could damage the ozone.

Tests showed that a single chlorine atom could destroy tens of thousands of ozone molecules. It had taken a scientific team twenty years to figure out that chlorine, broken out of its compound by sunlight, was damaging the ozone layer. So it became an assault on two fronts—a weakened ozone layer and an attack of pernicious chlorine gas. There was a rush to cope with the problem that Cayce may have applauded. Led by the U.S., fifty-seven nations agreed to cut the chlorine use to half-strength, and to halt production of the noxious chemicals altogether by the Millennium. The U.S. delegation to the Montreal conference concluded that the ozone layer was essential to life on Planet Earth.

The *Los Angeles Times* noted that the ozone layer, monitored by scientists, had diminished three times faster than expected in twelve years, from 1985 to 1997. Scientists estimated that this could translate into two hundred thousand deaths from skin cancer in fifty years.

Just before his death in 1945, Edgar Cayce predicted the ozone problem would gradually fade away as the errant pole returned to its original home. Physicist McDonald gives the ozone layer another two thousand years, with constantly diminishing protection from the sun, before the magnetic field fades out and another begins to take its place.

Edgar Cayce didn't look that far ahead. He saw the beginning of a rising consciousness that will bring man into Millennial harmony with his God in the ceaseless struggle for survival and fulfillment.

Cayce summed it up as he had before: "'As ye sow, so shall ye reap,' was said two thousand years ago by the One who comes again. It was never more true than now when His presence shall again grace our day."

As for the sun, Cayce was very much aware of its communication with stubborn, irreconcilable man. To whom he spoke in biblical language:

"Be honest with thyself, as ye would ask even the ruler of this earth—the sun—to hearken to the voice of that which created it and gives its light irrespective of how ye act. For, as given, the sun shineth upon the just and the unjust alike, yet it is oft reflected in what happens to thee in thy journey through life.

"The more ye become aware of thy relationship to the Universe and those influences that control man, the greater thy ability to help, to aid, the greater to rely upon the force within. But still greater, thy responsibility to thy fellow man. For as ye do unto the least, ye do it unto thy Maker. Even as to the sun which reflects the turmoils that arise within thee. Even as the earthquake, and the wars and hates, even as the influences in thy life day by day.

"So what you ask, are the sun spots? What do they have to do with us? Simply told, they are a natural consequence of that turmoil which the sons of man in the earth darken the heavens. Thus they bring confusion to those who become aware of the sun's closeness to God. Let not your heart be troubled. Yet believe in God. Then act like it—to others. He has given thee a mind, a body, and a land in which to dwell. He has set the sun, the moon, the planets, the stars about thee to remind thee, even as the psalmist gave, 'Day unto day uttereth speech, night unto night sheweth knowledge.'

"As what does thy soul appear? A spot, a blot upon thy sun? Or as that which giveth light unto those who sit in darkness, to those who cry aloud for hope? Hast thou created hope in thy association with thy fellow man? Ye fear and cringe when ye find that the spots upon thy sun cause confusion of any nature.

"How must thy Savior feel, look, appear, when ye

deny Him day by day, when ye treat thy fellow man as though he were as dross and trash before thee?"

The answer for man, Cayce found, was simple: "Shape up, and know thyself."

Chapter Five
World Affairs

Edgar Cayce would have made a great secretary of state. He had God the Creator as his Prime Minister and Jesus as God's spokesman. Communing with these advisers over the years, he had foreseen the end of Godlessness in the two most powerful Godless countries in the world: the Soviet Union and the People's Republic of China.

When Cayce said Russia will be "the hope of the world" the Russian churches were shuttered and Stalin, the anti-Christ, had made it a crime for his millions of subjects to worship the Lord. Cayce's followers sighed and shook their heads.

But they reckoned without Cayce's Prime Minister. Stalin, the despot who kept Russia in chains, died suddenly after World War II, some thought mysteriously, and the Communist state began to unravel. Huge provinces like Ukraine left the mother country, and the people, hiding their Bibles for years, renewed their worship of Jesus and the Father. Finally, the Iron Curtain was lifted. The new Russian government assumed ties with the West, and the threat of a nuclear war abated. With Cayce seeing no such war well beyond the Millennium.

Cayce went on with his prophecy. "This hope was not as that termed of the Communistic or the Bolshevistic. But of freedom, freedom! That each man will live for his fellow man. It will take years for the principle to be crystallized, but out of Russia," he repeated, "comes the hope of the world."

Guided, as Cayce saw, by ties with the United States. "That friendship with the nation that hath as its present monetary unit the expression 'In God we trust.'"

Cayce added a wry aside: "Do you use that in thine own heart when you pay your just debts? Or in the prayer when you send thy missionaries to other lands?"

He deplored the Japanese attacks in another generation on the Chinese mainland. "Rather should the principles of the Christian faith be carried forward in and through the turmoils that are a part of both China and Japan."

The Chinese could hardly appreciate this coupling with the country raining bombs on their cities. But Cayce, as usual, held that the merchants of death were as much victims of the bombings as those who were killed. For this was something they would have to deal with for the rest of their lives.

As China's trials and tribulations continued, with the Japanese extending their attacks, millions in an awakening China looked to a new God for understanding and help in dealing with the tragedies that befell them and their families. Cayce suffered, too, as his subconscious mind viewed the desolation and despair of the stricken.

There seemed no end to the wars and power struggles ending finally in the triumph of the Communists over the armies of Chiang-Kai-shek. With a government, like its Russian counterpart, not paying homage to God.

But China would awaken one day. Cayce said, "There are those conditions arising from this great emptiness in the consciousness of many that will bring the revolution [bloodless] in the minds of many peoples and begin that understanding of the gift of God in the One made manifest in the flesh."

At a time when foreigners were taboo in China, Cayce visualized its people cutting off the ponytails by which they were figuratively raised to heaven to join their ancestors, eventually becoming a force in world affairs and moving closer to Christianity. More than sixty years ago he saw a country with more than a billion people, wedded to Buddhism and Taoism, coming out of its isolation to one day contemplate, despite its Communist leadership, the teachings of Jesus Christ:

"There was a growth of heart and mind, a powerful

stream through a land which for ages asked to be left alone, to be satisfied with that in itself. Then it awoke one day and cut its hair off [the ponytails]. It began to think of the world that had made itself felt, and it began to do something with its thinking. And with this thinking will evolve one day and become, as unlikely as it may seem, the cradle of Christianity as applied to the lives of man. Yea, it is far off as man counts time, but only a day in the heart of God. For tomorrow China will awake and know God. Not the God of its fathers but the God of itself. And will become a powerful force in the peace of the world."

Some of China's growing bond to the Christian faith had been stirred by the wracking pains of the Japanese attacks on its mainland and in part by the bruising civil war in which the Communists and Mao climbed to power. Who can forget the picture on the front pages across the world of a sobbing young mother holding the broken body of her small child in her arms amid the ruins of a city shattered by a Japanese aerial attack?

Cayce saw the advent of Christianity in China and its creed of forgiveness, easing some of the pain and bringing a new resolve to a nation that has yet to stretch its muscles to their full extent. A nation, he said, that would one day join with the U.S. in maintaining the peace.

Cayce became even more engrossed with China as he neared the end of his life. He was very much aware of the global potential of this giant of the Eastern world, intent, serious, hardworking, believing in themselves and country, as they chose a Christian life, even though the word Christianity itself would not be in approved usage for a good many years.

Cayce was questioned frequently about the Chinese, for that country traditionally had been viewed sympathetically by an America responding to the needs of children so often the victims of famines and orphaned in wars that surged around them. He was encouraged by what he saw, a nation ever closer to God:

"Much might be said as to the various sects in China at the present time. But these will be united more and more, toward the Democratic way. Just as it has begun and it has been the last twenty years. And it will grow and spread faster in the next twenty-five, and more in the last five, than in the first ten.

"More and more will those of the Christian faith come to be in political positions, and this in China will mean the greater rule in certain groups, according to how well these manifest. And these will progress. For Civilization and its influence moves west with the Millennium."

This was an old thesis of Cayce's, the westward trend of the dominant culture, with the mantle eventually falling on the U.S., and intrinsically its westernmost state of California, which has become the world's leading communication center with a grip on the motion picture and television world.

The Sleeping Prophet would have been pleased by reports coming out of a burgeoning China twenty-five years after his death in 1945, the year of his predicted ending of World War II.

He had also predicted that China would open its doors to American political leaders, industrialists, and even the Christian clergy. Not to mention President Nixon and a host of American reporters. One of these, James (Scotty) Reston of the *New York Times*, appeared to be impressed by what he saw. "Although the Chinese [the Communist leaders] would be the first to deny that there are religious overtones to their propaganda and ideology, the similarities to the Protestant ethic are unmistakable."

Every morning a mimeographed report in English was delivered at Reston's door in a Beijing Hotel, with a quotation from Chairman Mao Tse-tung, not only chairman of China's Communist Party, but of 1.3 billion Chinese men, women and children. Instead of a corroding comment on the evils of capitalism, Reston was surprised to find a morality lesson. Not as sweeping as the Ten Commandments, but still covering a wide range of human behavior.

"We just learn the spirit of absolute selflessness," said Mao. "Diligence, frugality and modesty. Remember these three."

Enumerated were "The eight points for attention," each the equivalent of a commandment:

1. Speak politely.
2. Pay fairly for what you buy.
3. Return everything you borrow.
4. Pay for anything you damage.
5. Do not hit or swear at people.
6. Do not damage crops.
7. Do not take liberties with women.
8. Do not ill-treat captives.

Like so many visitors to China, Reston was impressed by the young, busily working in fields and shops, seeming to enjoy their labor in the oldest civilization in the world. He saw a thousand young men and women cheerfully building a highway, digging the earth out of hills with picks and shovels, and carrying it in baskets to the new road. Everyone seemed to be enjoying what they were doing. Building a new China they hoped would be theirs one day.

The aboriginal lure for religion that would bring one closer to a superspirit, namely God, entranced the young Chinese, as it did the young in every land since Moses announced to his people there was a living God and He was one and all-powerful. Even more important than Mao, if you were to summon this reality, and dared to voice it. Mao, being wiser than Stalin and Hitler, was not about to compete with God, as Cayce saw, only angling to keep Him in the background.

Reston, an unusually astute reporter, looked deep into a young China's heart. He saw no religious fervor, only a quiet and steadfast resolve to make a better and stronger nation, with a transcending belief in a Higher Power.

It is something that enlightened Puritans like Emerson and Thoreau would have recognized at once. For the work ethic had many coattails, the principal one being the Creator, without whom there would be no coattails.

Cayce was intrigued by China, not only by its bigness, but its challenge to Christianity. As an ardent Christian, Cayce would have liked nothing more than to see the Chinese as Presbyterians (his Sunday school class), Baptists, Methodists or any other Christian church that taught the young to be dutiful and useful and keep all the Commandments.

He influenced many seekers to visit China, as he felt that America could have a moderating influence on that awesome giant and in return affect the visitors' religious and work ethic.

Curious visitors poured into China, as Cayce noted, from all over the world, some to help, others to observe and to learn. Some came because of Cayce, intrigued by what he said of China becoming a landmark for Christianity. It seemed almost unbelievable, despite the corps of Christian clergymen converting Chinese to Christianity before the Communist takeover.

Thirty years after Cayce's death his prophecies were being played out by travelers looking for some signs of the Christianity Cayce had laid out so plainly. One of these visitors, Dr. Gultelan Caymaz, a medical doctor from Ankara, Turkey, spent weeks during advanced medical studies in China looking into Edgar Cayce's predictions of the growth of Christianity in the People's Republic. He found they were true.

He was accompanied by another medical doctor and a nurse. They had been invited to study acupuncture, anesthesia and therapy. "While doing this study," he said, "we naturally observed the moral, religious practices of the people in general.

"The nurse was my late wife, an American Catholic. The other doctor and myself were Muslims. We all believed in God and our religious teachings, basically the same as Christianity."

The Chinese people he met, generally, said they did not believe in God, nor did they believe in survival after death. "Yet their practice of moral ethics was high, higher than what we observed in the U.S., Europe, Muslim countries, and such places as Hong Kong, the Philippines, Japan, and Taiwan."

They saw people invariably courteous to each other. Kind and gentle. There was no noise in the streets. No trash. No fights or arguments. No beggars. No prostitution. They asked questions and saw that everybody was given work. Nobody was left hungry. Everybody had similar shirts, skirts (below the knee) or trousers. They were clean and washed. Not shredded at the knees like our blue jeans. The women didn't use makeup or lipstick. There was no sign of luxury.

The doctor found them a friendly people. They talked openly about their religious convictions. He thought them contradictory. "One day I told our interpreter that even though you declare that you don't believe in God or the soul you Chinese people obey God's teachings and practice religious rules. The most stringent in the world, stopping prostitution, giving everybody work, to earn a living according to their abilities, practicing humbleness, wearing no sexy clothes, frowning on adultery, being unselfish, and practicing brotherhood, advocated by Jesus and the Muslim faith."

He believed the People's Republic was unique in its attitude about religion. "It is the only country practicing religion among its people while not professing they are religious or believe in God."

His relations with the Chinese medical fraternity, in helping the sick, were impressive. "No act of selfishness or superiority toward my colleague and myself was evident though our hosts were making major medical discoveries and offering them to the world. They were modest, and taught humility. 'Whatever we accomplished,' they said, 'we accomplished while seeking to relieve the suffering of patients.' When we expressed our gratitude for what they were teaching us, they responded, 'We are just exchanging views with you. We learn from each other. We are not teaching you anything. Make your suggestions, tell us our mistakes so we can be more helpful to humanity.' "

While appreciating the work ethic and the friendliness, Dr. Caymaz did see some cracks in the system. "In China if your personal ideas don't agree with the government policies, you may be sent away to work for years without seeing your family. There is no freedom of travel for people such as us without written permission. However, I believe some of these restrictions are due to economic difficulties. As the economy eases, I think there will be more freedom for recreation and travel. Many countries with economic problems have similar restrictions. But dwelling on these financial restrictions seems quite selfish when so many people around the world are suffering from poverty, sickness or hunger."

There were greater imponderables, encompassing more than China.

Like so many, I ruminated over something Cayce had said and what so many of us thought on different occasions. It was nothing earthshaking, but it was about the core of life and it did make one think. "What," asked Cayce of himself, "what is life all about?"

I hastily turned the page and read on from the wisdom of Cayce's Universal Intelligence. It was something I had heard many times and that I would ponder anew. It said it all:

"Thou shalt love thy God with all thine heart, thine soul, thine mind, thine body, and thy neighbor as thyself. The rest of all the theories that may be concocted by man are as nothing, if just these are lived. Love thy neighbor as thyself day by day, as did the Christ who died on the Cross that others might live with Him forever."

It would have been a poetic ending, even if Cayce had not added: "Know then that as He had His Cross, so have you. May you take it with a smile. You can, if you will let Him bear it with thee."

I wondered what Mao Tse-tung would have thought.

Since the visit of the Turkish doctors, much has happened in China. The doors have been flung open to American business. McDonald's, the hamburger king, has been allowed to open forty stores in Beijing. Coca-Cola franchises are popping up in China's largest cities. The missionaries have been doing better. The Mormon Church, into the work ethic, conservative in approach to its members' lifestyle, has carved a niche of its own in a country where the work ethic is equally strong and frivolity deplored.

Cayce's subconscious wandered afar. It frequently turned to India, a land for which he felt a chord of sympathy because of its belief in reincarnation, which had become a cornerstone of his life and that of his family. Asked about India's struggle for independence, Cayce stated that Gandhi, India's spiritual leader, had a greater force supporting him than all the English king's men: nonresistance.

"In time it will weaken the English position, as England in the world's eyes will loom as a bully tormenting a helpless old lady. Great Britain is losing an excellent fight. Non-resistance is hard to beat."

He had some misgivings about India's future under self-rule. "As to whether those peoples will remain, or whether the prayers and supplications of others will be heeded depends on individuals. In India the cradle of knowledge is not applied, except within self. What is the sin of India? Self, and leaving the 'ish' off—just self."

Not until the total obliteration of India's pernicious caste system—not only in law but in the hearts of man—did he see a free India basking in the light of freedom.

He was concerned, above all, with his own country—America the Beautiful, rugged, ambitious, yet generous and warmhearted. A country often divided by race and religion, yet caring for the homeless, the underdog, the aged and the infirm.

He would close his eyes and question his Universal

Intelligence. "Is America fulfilling its destiny? Is it filling its place as a nation? What, my children, have ye done with the knowledge that ye have respecting the relationships of thy Creator to thy fellow man? And hast thou made known that ye know of His ways, God's ways, among thy fellows? Yea, here and there as you have seen, America has become the fusion of many different cultures, which helps, as it were, to leaven the whole."

Elsewhere, he stressed that brotherhood was necessary for the United States to continue as the land of the free and the home of the brave.

And then he got into the Millennium. "And here, there, as given, His messenger shall appear. Finding those that make the path straight."

Warning repeatedly of riots in the streets, he stressed they could lead to chaos unless there was a love of country by the rioters and the power brokers. "For all have the same responsibility to see the country prosper with, as a great leader said, 'Government of the people, by the people, for the people.'"

He saw problems with big labor getting as big or bigger than big capital, strutting about showing its muscles.

I was tuning in on all this when a stormy United Parcel Service strike broke. I wondered whether Cayce's antenna had reached out and scanned what I was putting on paper. The strike dragged on and affected millions of people. I listened to abrasive exchanges between the company and its striking union, then went on to what Cayce had to say about peace between labor and capital:

"While needed demands are being made by labor and capital, there may be worked out that which can bring better relationships. Else there will come such divisions as to cause a general uproar and the need for legislation to control same. So long as there is not a united labor," added America's greatest psychic, "there may be dealings with capital. The greater troubles are those that might arise from a united labor against capital."

As a onetime unionist (the Newspaper Guild) I blinked. Then remembered the three great newspapers killed by a printers' strike. It was a sad day for America. And newspaper people everywhere.

Chapter Six
The Death Ray

The Sleeping Prophet awakened from a deep trance one day to learn that he had predicted that a Death Ray, such as he visualized in fabled Atlantis, would be produced in this country in twenty-five years.

Cayce had already left this earth plane when the scientists at a University of California, Berkeley, laboratory came up with a super-cosmic ray bringing in the pre-Millennial Age. It was called the Death Ray: forecast in 1933, conceived in 1958.

To be activated, a laserlike proton beam had to come together with a stream of antineutrons to develop the necessary antiprotons, to produce a tremendous energy. There was no evidence the resulting beam had been applied in our society. Obviously, if used and effective, there would have been little to show for it. The announcement of the ray was followed by an academic blackout a Death Ray couldn't pierce.

Other scientists saw the possibilities of combining antineurons and antiprotons, whatever they are, to convert matter into energy, disposing of the problem, whether a dinosaur or a creaky building. But by this time the atomic bomb had displaced the Death Ray as a twentieth-century horror story.

The Cayce prediction came out of a virtual blackout. It had developed from a question by the seer's son, Hugh Lynn Cayce, who was investigating stories of a Great Earth Congress to map plans for the destruction of the eighty-ton dinosaurs that once roamed the planet.

Cayce saw clearly that the people of that primitive period had no weapons available to handle the monsters that were overrunning the land and foraging to save themselves from extinction.

The answer, he saw, was in prayer to the Almighty to give them the insight and power to overcome this menace they couldn't fight with the raw iron and stones that were their only weapons. Looking back thousands of years, he told his son:

"In the period when this became necessary, there was the consciousness raised in the minds of the groups, in various portions of the earth, much in the manner as would be illustrated by an all-world broadcast in the present day of a menace in any one particular point, or in many particular points. And the gathering of those that heeded, as would be the scientific minds of the present day, in devising ways and means of doing away with that particular kind or class of menace. As to the manner in which these gathered, it was very much as it would be if the GrafZeppelin [an ill-fated German dirigible] were to gather those that were to counsel, and to cooperate in that effort. And this was in that particular plane or sphere in a land which has long since lost its identity."

And so these men of a simple nature went deep within themselves and prayed to the spirit in the heavens, the Creator, and the sun they worshiped him by, for the help they could find nowhere else. For prayer was the only weapon they had in so unequal a struggle, and the sun, with its light and heat, was their avenue to the Lord, as it was to so many of the natives Columbus found when he discovered America.

How was it to be done? In a very ingenious way, obviously with heavenly help, for in no other way could it have been achieved. Just as Cayce said again and again that with the Lord man can achieve anything, and without him there are only continuing upheavals of the earth and endless contention and wars reflected in the eruptions within the bowels of the earth.

It was the Lord, said Cayce, who showed them how to use the sun to make the cosmic rays that kept his favorite creatures (best known to Himself) from being wiped out by the roving bands of eighty-ton monsters. Their prayers were heeded as Cayce describes:

"Man has ever, even as then, when in distress, either mental, physical or spiritual, sought to know his connection with the divine force that brought the worlds

into being. As these are sought, so does the promise
hold true, that giveth man from the beginning, 'Will ye
be my children, I will be thy God. Ye turn your face
from me, my face is turned from thee. And those things
you have builded in thine own endeavor to make manifest thine own powers bring those certain destructions
in the lives of individuals in the present, even as in
those first experiences with the use of those powers
that are so taboo by the worldly wise, that are looked
upon as old men's tales and women's fables. Yet in the
strength of such forces do Worlds come into being.' ''

Cayce was again alluding to the power of prayer,
which such scientists as Einstein and Newton understood so well, knowing enough to know that the immensity of a world that transcended time and space
could only have been born of a Divine force that inter-
ceded only when man seemed on the verge of destroying himself.

"And that force," as Cayce said, "was exemplified
by what the psychic force did mean, has meant, and
does mean in the world today."

With this force, Cayce said, helped by the Lord,
primitive man was able to reach a higher consciousness where he employed crystals to capture the explosive power of the sun and direct the rays at various
stations at the hordes of trumpeting monsters bent on
taking over the earth.

Even greater monsters, Cayce said in 1936, would
soon begin their war against the civilized world, but
they would be two-legged monsters, with the promise

again given by the Lord that they would be destroyed in turn.

In other ages, some prehistoric humans invading the fabled continent of Atlantis, traveling through space were able to destroy that portion of the continent over which the Sargasso Sea presently floats. These people of Atlantis, according to Cayce, had lost the support of the Creator with their licentious and greedy lives, their lust for power, their disregard of the Almighty who had advanced them in their status.

It was, said Cayce, the first atomic war. "The individuals [the invaders] being able to raise the powers from the sun itself, to the ray that makes for the disintegration of the atom, brought about the destruction in that portion of the land, now presented, or called the Sargasso Sea.

"With the subsequent destruction in Atlantis, the secret of manipulating the sun in the disintegration of the atom was lost. In this falling back on a power of self, some other self presumed to be of greater power than God Himself was destroyed."

The closest thing to a Death Ray prior to its discovery in a California laboratory resulted from a Columbia University professor's research into the increase in cosmic ray energy, accounting in part for global warming. Professor Bruce Heezen, a true scientist, didn't delve into the harnessing of such energies for weapons of mass destruction. Some of which has been carried on by others and has now entered the military mainstream, where it is talked about in whispers behind locked doors.

Something akin to the Cayce Death Ray was described as a "particle beam weapon" which sends energy into the atomic structure of the target, causing the electrons to shift about. By releasing more energy than the inanimate target can absorb, this causes the target's molecules to come apart in a thermal explosion. This is another high-frequency energy weapon known among the cognoscenti or insiders as the Star Wars technology.

Some wondered whether this was similar to the killer weapon Cayce said was employed with the help of sun-magnetized crystals to demolish the dinosaurs that once romped around Atlantis.

In Heezen's research he cited mass extinctions resulting from a shift in the magnetic field, including the vulnerable ozone hole, through which the ultraviolet rays of the sun, described as a shimmering ball of atomic power, bombarded the unwitting earth people.

Heezen described his findings at a congress of more than one thousand scientists sponsored by UNESCO and the Soviet government in a New Age display of international amiability such as Cayce had foreseen. Heezen explained that when the earth's magnetic field reverses there is a period, as it reverses poles, when the electromagnetic field around the earth appears. That last reversal of the magnetic field was seven hundred thousand years ago. At the present time the magnetic field is decreasing, subjecting the earth to the cosmic bombardment Cayce warned about.

It would take a Cayce to understand how the scientists could bandy all these Millenniums around as if they were so many minutes. Some of the scientists were baffled as well, with the press staggered more by the grand scope of the heavens than a Cayce prediction of Christ's return for His birthday.

"The analysis of rock cores extracted from the floors of the Atlantic, Pacific and Indian Oceans provided proof of the magnetic reversals," said the head of Columbia's Lamont Geological Observatory. But with science so frequently falling back on assumptions dealing with phenomena occurring a million years ago, and a million miles away, it was easily understood why few but Cayce understood the reversal of the earth's magnetic field. That was the way the Creator planned it. It was an orderly process that man had more to do with than he thought.

And as Cayce elaborated: "Man has ever [even then] when in distress sought to know his association, his connection, with the divine forces that brought the worlds into being. As these are sought, so does the promise hold true, given from the beginning:

" 'Will ye be my children, I will be thy God. Ye turn your face from me, my face is turned from thee, and those things you have builded in thine own endeavor to make manifest thine own powers bring those certain destruction in the lives of individuals in the present, even as in those first experiences with the use of those powers that are so taboo with the worldly-wise, that are looked upon as old man's tales and woman's fables. Yet in the strength of such forces do worlds come into being.' "

The scientists didn't follow Cayce any more than he

followed them. But a handful of scientists, including
Professor Heezen, believed that excessive bombardment of cosmic rays, passing through gaping holes in
the magnetic field's ozone layer, were capable of causing genetic mutations leading to a new species of life.
Evoking such heavy blasts of cosmic rays they trig-
gered the extinction of some species—including the
rampaging dinosaurs.

Besides a Death Ray, Cayce foresaw all kinds of
low-level light beams, lasers, which could be used in
medicine and warfare. Before the Millennium, as recently as 1997, the U.S. Air Force was testing the striking power of beams of light from lasers at moving
targets, primarily orbiting satellites in space. Which
Cayce described.

The six-foot-wide beam of light from the laser was
able to track the satellite and illuminate it, a nice way
of saying it destroyed its target. The tests were held at
the Air Force base in White Sands, New Mexico, amid
gossip that the Defense Department's heavy-duty laser,
prophetically named the Miracle, could be a killer ray.

The Defense Department was quick to dispel reports
of a destroyer out of Mars or Atlantis—or a Cayce
reading. The tests were being held, officials said, to
check the vulnerability of our satellites to laser strikes,
deliberate or inadvertent, not as offensive weapons
against any other power.

Cayce foreshadowed light beams later used in healing. He spoke of radionics, used in color therapy, and
an etheronic analyzer, checking any disharmony in the
human body.

Radionics, originally mentioned by Cayce, was developed by a San Francisco physician. He theorized that diseases could be diagnosed by evaluating radiation from the human body. Support for radionics—and Cayce—came from Professor William Tiller, chairman of material science at Stanford University. He saw promise in color therapy: "There is Soviet work going on at this moment in which they are shining laser beams at acupuncture points. And depending on the wavelengths they use, they are producing healing modalities. They're getting strong effects of recuperation in people for a whole variety of conditions, but it depends on the color combinations they use. In this particular case laser light."

Things are moving so fast in the pre-Millennial period we often take change for granted. Ours is the age of computer communication, satellite programming, fiber optics, instant-access cable. Our VCRs are voice-programmable, our grocery checkout lines scan prices with lasers, and a wafer-thin computer disk contains the fourteen thousand Edgar Cayce readings. Whether it's medicine, technology, ecology or biology, the world is very different from what it was fifteen or twenty years ago, let alone six or seven decades ago, when Cayce was predicting all these things and more.

Long before television was no more than a wink in the inventor's eye, Cayce saw it clearly on the screen of his mind. He saw it first in the advanced technology of Atlantis: "Where there was the storage, as it were of the motivative forces in nature from the great crystals that so condensed the lights, the forms, the activities as to guide not only the ship upon the bosom of the sea but in the air and many of those now known conveniences for man as in the transmission of the body, and of the voice, as in the recording of those activities in what is soon to become a practical thing in so creating the vibrations as to make for television."

He was asked, "How long will be the period of popular development?"

"In the next fifteen years."

He had years before predicted the popularity of another magic development—a radio without wires of any sort.

"How," he asked, "will the television affect the radio?"

He saw a lag in television for the wrong reasons. "Dependent upon how easily those who have investments of such an extent are willing to allow television to take its place." Mainly the radio interests, fearful television would supplant radio. Cayce saw both living together as they had before. The first radio, like the first television set, he said, was invented in Atlantis, and placed for the first time in North America in Yucatán, brought to this continent by the Atlanteans. "Establishing the temple through which there was hoped to be the appearance again of the children of the Law of One [new Atlantean migrants] as they listened to the oracles that came through the stones, the crystals, that were prepared for communications in what ye know as radio."

This gave me a bit of a start. The first radio I had owned as a boy was called a crystal set.

In 1936 Cayce was asked what investments were best for the next few years.

"Those that have to do with communications when considered for years." Which predictions would have enriched those who used this advice to invest in the high-tech stocks featured in the bullish stock markets of the 1990s, including the industries tied in with computers and the Internet.

Again he stressed: "The industrials having to do with communications of all natures for long term."

He showed more restraint, though equal foresight, when three years before the outbreak of World War II in Europe he put on his immediate buy list: "Those stocks that are of allied industrials that deal with preparation of war materials for the next few months."

He had a prolonged interest in the communications industry, having said that as long as people and nations kept their communication lines open, peace would reign among diverse peoples and nations.

"In the study, in the preparation for the mental and material advancement in communications," he said as early as 1934, "especially as to those relationships that we find should be as fact in a few years, the united activity of radio and the telegraph lines. This is indicated by the field of activity through the radiograms from communications in the distant portions not only from vessels at sea but land communications handled in pretty much the same manner."

The merging of the communications systems, predicted by Cayce, resulted in the International Telecommunications systems, noted by a popular magazine thirty years later under the headline: "From Telepathy to Space Communications in 100 years."

Cayce foresaw international broadcasts by television and then went on to say there would be communications with the planets, realized when the United States put its astronauts on the moon and began to contact Mars and the other planets.

The world would become a place where the most distant peoples would exist, electronically, as next-door neighbors, sharing their problems, helping or hindering according to our consciousness. Cayce stressed that people working together, in the same cause, could raise the energy and thought to a spiritual level. Some of the physical earth changes mentioned decades ago by Cayce could not be changes on a different level, with the positive energy of millions, even billions, of earthlings beginning to visualize the Creator as a very real power behind this awesome Universe of ours.

While incidental quakes and floods are part of the earth's normal evolution, potentially greater changes could come, Cayce said, from worldwide political turmoil, depressions, wars, ecological disasters, and climatic changes—subject to the changes he saw in man's energy. "God proposeth, man disposeth.

"Our personal upheavals," said Cayce, "are not necessarily geological in nature. As to the changes that are coming, these will, as indicated, depend on what individuals and groups do about what they know respecting His will, His purpose with man."

So many of the positive changes foreseen by Cayce were being reaffirmed almost daily by people massing together, showing a higher consciousness, such as the peaceful convocations of Christians in Washington dedicating themselves to brotherhood beyond the restraints of their own churches. For didn't Jesus, a recurring emblem of Christianity, say that he was not only the shepherd to His flock but to those outside the flock? And there were the black women, emulating their men, gathering in a peaceable way reaffirming their dedication to the dignity and freedom of womanhood under God.

The newspapers were full of the one-world consciousness that Cayce deemed essential to the existence of a civilized society. We are now allies and friends with nations we once fought. The collapse of Communism in Europe, and in China moderation, the European Economic Community bound with the awareness that we must come together as one planet to heal the ecological, environmental world we call our own. Cayce's most provocative predictions were not about earthquakes, but about a new world being born, taking off with this Millennium. The changes he saw provided an opportunity to get our priorities in focus. They were not a single event but an ongoing process. The promise of the New Age was a promise of change. The earth changes of the past were experienced, as Cayce noted, as an omen of our need for a greater global community.

While the usual conflicts of smaller nations for scraps of land persisted, there was a worldwide trend, as Cayce saw, toward diverse people working together. The United Nations adopted standards covering economic regulations, nuclear energy, human rights, pollution controls, customs procedures—even space law.

"Moving to a One-World Society," read a current newspaper headline. Moving slowly, to be sure, with the usual flare-ups in the Middle East, Ireland, the Balkans, Bosnia, with incursions in Africa. But as Cayce stressed, the one-world, one-fate consciousness was growing. Even the most xenophobic or closed-off peoples were aware they could no longer avoid disaster by shutting down their physical and emotional borders. We were all in the same pot together—and had better tolerate, if not like each other. While catching on to the reality of a Creator who wasn't purely a fancy of man, but a force to be reckoned with in every level of our lives.

Chapter Seven
The Atlanteans

Just as he saw a Communist Russia lifting the Iron Curtain and joining the family of nations, Cayce saw the Atlanteans returning to solid earth to become a friendly force in world affairs by the time the Millennium rolls around.

Cayce knew little about Atlantis early in the Twentieth Century. His conscious mind was very much occupied with his family and friends in his study groups in the Virginia Beach Tidewater area, which he pronounced the safest place in the country.

As the Millennium drew closer, visions of Atlantis began to flow through him. He saw a struggle for control of a vast and powerful empire between two bitterly warring factions—the self-indulgent, race-proud, sensuous Sons of Belial and the more spiritual Sons of the Law of One. It was a struggle increasingly bitter with the centuries, each side vying to win mastery of the earth with lethal weapons, stemming out of advance technologies dealing with atomic energy and powerful solar rays.

Cayce visualized it all in a few stark words, describing an end to a civilization that was far advanced to ours technologically. Whose weapons of destruction exceeded ours, even to the atom and hydrogen bombs.

"These forces," Cayce said, "were not only the rays from the sun, set by the facets of the firestones as crystallized from the heat from within the elements of the earth itself, but were as the combination of these. The use of these influences by the Sons of Belial brought then the first of the upheavals, by the turning of the etheric rays from the sun—as used by the Sons of the Law of One for the conveniences as for light, heat and electrical combinations—into the facet for the activities of same that produced volcanic upheavals of such widespread proportions that it caused the separating of the land into separate islands. Five in number."

And thus the Lost Continent became the continent of lost souls.

Cayce had never heard of Plato, the ancient Greek philosopher who was the first to write about a Lost Continent presumably destroyed, with its remains submerged in the Atlantic. Nor had Cayce ever read about Atlantis. He was too busy with his Bible, which he read every day, and the metaphysical readings he gave in his sleep. His first reading on Atlantis was as much of a surprise as his first reading on reincarnation, shocking to a fundamentalist Baptist who taught Sunday School in a Presbyterian church.

He was in a quandary. With his wife, Gertrude, he thumbed through the New Testament. He found a passage where the apostles asked Jesus if he was the prophet Elijah reborn. Jesus replied this was John the Baptist, saying they had taken John's life as they would His. Cayce's interest in reincarnation was quickened when he saw something that hadn't struck him earlier in the Bible: Paul saying that if one man was resurrected, all were.

The Atlantis visions began to take on new significance. They poured out of his subconscious mind. He saw hundreds of Atlanteans returning to a planet they had fled thousands of years ago, ready now for a new life, in a Millennium with storied memories and high expectations.

The early Cayce readings on Atlantis revealed a highly technical culture that deteriorated because of the people's rampant greed and lust for power, turning them from the protection of the Creator they knew as the Law of One. They became victims of their own self-indulgence. And Cayce saw the danger of man repeating the Atlantis disaster.

The geologists and archeologists ridiculed Cayce's Atlantis, just as they had sneered at the existence of ancient Troy as an old wives' tale. But a solid-thinking international businessman, Heinrich Schliemann, hardly a scientist, dug up the remains of a fabled civilization out of Homer's stories of the Trojan-Greek

wars, *The Iliad* and *The Odyssey,* and followed the trail
of the ancient poet to the buried city, locating not only
one but seven Troys.

With the Millennium approaching, numbers of people were heeding the renowned mystic who had gone
where the scientists feared to tread. Yet Atlantis is still
very much a mystery. From fossil remains, from layers
of earth crust, we know the earth goes back millions of
years. And yet we have little insight into what happened only yesterday geologically. Had some cata-
clysm, destroying much of humanity, destroyed the
records of that humanity? Which, Cayce said, were
preserved in the sacred tombs of the pyramids, in the
ancient land of Egypt, where so many of the Atlanteans, according to Plato, sought a new life. Others
turned up in Asia Minor and Latin America, with many
city names similar to those in the eastern Mediterranean—already named when the first explorers came
from Spain.

The Cayce readings state that if a geological survey
were made along the Gulf Stream near the Bahamian
Island of Bimini, concrete evidence of artifacts would
be found establishing rudiments of the Lost Continent.
Along with the debris of sunken barges and trucks,
searchers have located marble pillars and hexagon
pavements without getting to the ocean depth Cayce
advised. He saw remnants of Atlantis rising before the
Millennium. Dredging the channel of Bimini Bay recently, searchers did locate in shallow water some
freshwater mangrove peat about nine thousand years
old, signifying the land was above water at that time

for the mangrove trees to flourish. Indicating this was then a habitable land which Cayce saw as a remnant of the Lost Continent.

It was a very real Atlantis that Cayce visioned. Contemplating the destruction that took place in three distinct periods, he warned all this could happen again unless man considered the lessons of the past. Nevertheless, he foresaw a heightening consciousness of these perils, with a new flow of spirituality nourished by the Atlanteans reborn in the New Aquarian Age.

Cayce's fourteen thousand psychic readings indicate that some seven hundred of his subjects had incarnations in Atlantis, many of them bringing memories of the past into their new lives. Along with the burnished skills and knowledge of a superior technology. Many recounted lives during the three periods of geological change in Atlantis—50,000 B.C., 28,000 B.C., and 10,000 B.C. They brought their history with them, describing the angry rumbles of earthquakes and volcanoes that gave warnings of the breakup of the land, enabling them, Cayce said, to escape to the accessible Mediterranean area. Many settled in Egypt, others drifting to the islands of the Caribbean and the surrounding mainland, where in time they revealed an uncanny knowledge of physics, chemistry and electronics.

One boy was given a reading by Cayce when he was only eight because his parents were struck by his using an unknown variant of gunpowder to make his own fireworks. They were confused by Cayce mentioning a technical background in Atlantis, thinking he might be referring to Atlanta and Georgia Tech. As the boy went into junior high and then high school, he shone in chemistry and physics. His academic achievements in other areas were desultory. The parents were nevertheless skeptical when Cayce elaborated on the future of this eight-year-old in the electronics field.

"He became an electrical engineer," a Cayce follow-up revealed, "developing electronic installations that helped turn the tide for the Allies in the North African fighting of World War II. He was so quick to grasp the various technologies that he was given the opportunity in the middle of the war to work on the atom bomb."

He muddled over this for some time, his consciousness pricked by hazy recollections of a distant past when he was involved with the explosive forces that brought about the destruction of his former homeland.

His Cayce reading was something of a guide. Hazily recalling its destructive pattern in a past life when he worked with atomic energy, he decided he didn't want to renew the experience. He fought off the pressure to do the atomic work some thought best for the country. Ironically, later in the war, he was dispatched to the Atlantean area off Florida, where Cayce said he once lived. He had no feeling of nostalgia. There was a warning in the Cayce reading that he could be a constructive or destructive influence. Eventually, he chose the path that would give him a more serene but prosaic life, giving him the love of a caring woman. He was a model husband and father. What doubts he may have had were dispelled by his joy in producing a family with love and goodwill in their hearts. They thanked the Lord for the life given them, having avoided the horrors of a parent producing a bomb that leveled two Japanese cities.

Did he ever think back on Atlantis? Occasionally. He recalled having something to do with the molding of a firestone, by which atomiclike energy was created as the activity of the stone, as Cayce noted, was received from the sun's rays: "These then were impelled by the contraction of the rays from the stone centered in the middle of the power station or powerhouse [as would be termed in the present]. These, not intentionally, were tuned too high. And brought the second period of destructive forces to the Atlanteans, breaking up the land into isles when further destructive forces were brought in the land by the setting-up in various parts of the land that which was to produce the powers in many forms destructive to the cities, the towns, the countries surrounding same."

Cayce had gone on with the stone: "As to describing the construction of the stone, we find it was a large cylindrical glass cut with facets in such a manner that the capstone on top of same made for the centralizing of a force sufficient to erase any object or center. And this the boy grown into a man knew was something the Lord would not be pleased with."

Children with Atlantean backgrounds were uniformly advanced beyond their age. Some of the young women were of rare beauty. The Atlanteans were versed in health and beauty potions, exercise routines, and meditation under the auspices of the Law of One, with entrancing visions of the Body Beautiful.

In dealing with the transition from one life experience to another, Cayce noted that something of the spirit invariably remained to shape the inclinations and aspect of the currently incarnated person. Elder statesman Benjamin Franklin said of himself that he would come back like a book with a new cover, his age-old yearnings dotting the new pages.

There were many surprises in these Cayce readings touching on Atlantis. One mother from a wealthy family, concerned about her daughter, consulted Cayce with her equally concerned husband. Little did they know that they were to get a tour of Atlantis, with Egypt and the pyramids thrown in. They had heard stories of Cayce making the incurably sick well, advising people in the making of millions, telling authors how to write best-sellers. But they were only stories. The mother needed more, for her daughter's sake.

The daughter, Ginny, was precocious and pretty. Cayce described her to a T, as the parents marveled, and then pictured her as he saw her in Atlantis—bright, impulsive, beautiful: "Overactive in the physical and mental, one who in her early development could converse as well as individuals twice her age on the construction of automobiles, gas engines—having knowledge of fumigations for homes and drainages, for the better protection of health."

She had known lives in Egypt and "the Palestine land during those periods when the Master had walked the earth." The advanced life, the gentility and harmony of the teenager was attributed to an experience "as the child blessed by the Master; when he sayeth,

'Suffer little children to come unto me, and forbid them not. For such is the Kingdom of Heaven.' "

The parents were looking at each other, bewildered yet pleased. Their daughter blessed by Jesus. What could be better? Cayce reflected on his own remarks. "When a soul, then, has been blessed by Him, how may it ever wholly wander from that blessing as given by life itself? How when He—Christ—has promised in thine own experience that ye are to fill a purpose in the life of others? If ye will wholly trust in Him, then He and ye will not fail.

"Before that," Cayce went on, "the entity was in the land now known as the Atlantean, during those periods when destructive forces were imminent through the falling away of the people and the uprisings of the Sons of Belial."

She was of those believing in the Law of One—the Lord—using forces that inadvertently brought "bodily instruction [accounting for the teenager's facility with engines and other mechanical devices] yet rejecting the activities of those rebellious to the Law of One, finding those interests in things that have become a portion of the soul activity."

These were ideals, he said, still lingering in the sub-conscious of this idealistic and spiritual teenager about whom the mother was so concerned.

There were the usual queries as Cayce opened his eyes and smiled.

"What," asked the mother, "is the best way for her mother to handle the conditions that arise in her daughter's life?"

"Most by example. That there is an ideal, and that ideal must be in the spiritual life. That judgments in the moral, the commercial, the material, the mental may be judged by the One standard set by Him who blessed thy daughter in that far land."

The mother was also concerned with the physical, her daughter's growth. The girl was already as tall as her mother. "Is she growing too fast, and is there any way to keep her from being too tall?"

A wakened Cayce had no trouble with this. "It's the normal, natural development. Let there be sufficient of the correct exercising of the body to keep a normal balance in its development, with a systematic purposefulness."

As the mother persisted, I wondered how she would have felt had the daughter been too short. "How," she asked, "can one keep from being sensitive about being too tall?"

Cayce answered with equanimity, understanding a mother's concern about an impressionable daughter.

"Know that what has been builded by self is the expression of that which is best for what the soul has to do in this sojourn. This should, with this knowledge, remove all sensitivity, knowing that what is, is that which may be used for His glorification in the earth."

The mother understood the man she was questioning drew his power from the Universal Intelligence. She pursued her questioning.

"Please give any advice to the mother that will assist in making for the best development of this entity."

Cayce's response was surprising.

"Let a portion of the dress, either external or that close to the body, have something of blue. Keep not as a charm, but as the influences that may bring the greater force about the body. The moonstone or the bloodstone as the ornaments about the body, but those also to be found [that are akin to these] in the turquoise blue and the pigeon-blood ruby."

He paused a moment.

"As to advice to those that are responsible for the soul's environment: First know that not as a duty but as an opportunity has this soul been in thine own environ, not for self alone. But for the development of the soul that is in thine keeping, that this soul may bring to others much that will remind them oft that he gave, 'Of such is the kingdom of heaven.' "

He paused again, as if considering the wonders of birth entailed in a new soul, imbued with love, coming into being, needing all the love that could be mustered to navigate the rough and uncertain waters.

Cayce spoke of soulmates, young men and women in the halcyon days of Atlantis. Like so many in the present when the first bonding didn't succeed, they tried and tried again. Georgia, twice wed in the distant past as Cayce saw, was a junior executive this time around, pretty, much sought after, but confused whether she should stay on her job or get married.

"Get married," Cayce told her, "but be sure." For three times was the charm.

Cayce rarely acted as a marriage broker. But Georgia was compliant. He advised her to think back on how her soulmate relationship had failed. Too much attention to business.

"From the appearance as they affect the entity in the present and the indications as to the abilities of the entity in many fields of service. Especially in being of assistance in creating thinking in the minds of associates, we find that home gilding should be the business of the entity, as that time when the disturbances first began."

She should look back, said Cayce, and see how tending to business rather than her homework may have disrupted an Atlantean relationship she had thought arranged in heaven.

"Remember the manner of analyzing self as has been indicated. Look within. Judge or parallel what ye find with thy spiritual ideal. Not as to what you would desire others to be, but as to what ye desire to have others be to thee, that be to them. These are the manners in keeping with the proper material and mental relationships. The business side, as indicated, is of benefit in the helpfulness through instructions to many. But the home building should be the work, the life experience. For in this, and through the channels, may the great harmony come. As ye meet thyself in the material plane."

Georgia was still doubtful. She had carried a lot of baggage in Atlantis.

"Would marriage with this young man be advised, or should I wait for another?"

This, Cayce saw, was the same young man she had fretted over in two marriages in previous lives. But he saw a new opportunity in the current experience. As if her subconscious mind had relived it before and recognized, finally, that primary ingredient of life—a little thing called love.

"There should be the answer from within as to the purposes, the desires," said Cayce. "If the purposes of each act as a helpfulness one to another, WELL! If they do not, look for another. And unto yourself."

For this, then, would not be her soulmate. As he said so often, it should be the heart that controls the mind.

Still doubtful, she went on to the failed marriage in Atlantis. "What were the hurtful associations with my divorced husband? And why did things turn out as they did?"

Cayce replied, "In that experience when ye were led so far astray in Atlantis, then how could it have been any other way in the present? For the husband was the one who led the self astray in that experience. Again there were the meetings in the experience just before this [in Egypt], and these were not over helpful then, for they brought many disturbing conditions."

She was still groping, still looking into herself, as Cayce had suggested. "What," she asked, "were the lessons for me to learn in Atlantis?"

"That the spiritual things are to have their spiritual values and the material things their material values."

She looked at him doubtfully for a moment. Then, sighing, said as if testing him. For it wasn't very often that a young woman is told she shared two different lives with the same young man and was contemplating a third. Her eyes fell on the sleeping Cayce. It had been a long session and she was tired. But she had to be sure. Cayce had been so kind, so reassuring, so patient that she felt the least bit guilty as she asked, "Please give me the true local time of my present physical birth."

Cayce didn't hesitate. "This as we find was on the eighteenth at 2:33 P.M."

She smiled. It was all right now. There was no doubt. She knew what she had to do.

What a Millennium it would be.

Chapter Eight
Verna Comes Back

She remembers Atlantis as though it was only yesterday. She remembers the doctors and the chemists, the teachers and their students, the libraries and the museums. There were others, but these played the most vital role in her life. The leaders, the men who ruled over the people, lived in great castles and cared not about the people. She and her boyfriends were of the working class and spent their free hours in the libraries and the museums. For there was little other diversion as you lived within the Law of One or Belial. If you were of Belial you were of those who heeded no law but their own desire. And that was the great trouble, selfishness and greed and the lust for power. The rules were in Belial's hands. For they knew no power greater than their own and feared what they did not know—this God worshipped by those who lived within and for the Law of One. So few listened, for they found mere words fruitless. When they were warned of the One's wrath, they laughed and drank of the grape and feasted on the leanest part of the Unicorn, whom they sacrificed to their gods, the gods of licentiousness and greed, forgoing the commandments so long ago forgotten, telling the people to love one another. Or they would be lost, a Lost Continent, to which they could never return, for there would be nothing. Nothing, not even a flag in the soil where their homes and workplaces, their libraries and schools had once flourished under the Law of One.

This is the land Verna remembered. She remembered the good and the bad. For Atlantis had not always been corrupt. But like the land she had found refuge in, it had at one time loved the Creator whose Creation they were. And then when they grew fat and foolish with power they forgot who had made them great, until He turned away and it was too late. The planets no longer moved at their bidding, as when they listened to the Law of One. For some it was the end. But Verna had always remembered from whence she came, and the Lord remembered. He always remembered, just as He would remember His only begotten son as the Millennium rolled around again.

Verna liked it where she was. She had always devoured books where she was, and now she was a librarian in a small but friendly town outside the city of Chicago with its tall buildings and taller ambitions, its people so often too busy to stop and help a little old lady across the street. Something forgotten, too, by the people who no longer lived with the Law of One. But Verna remembered, for like President Harry Truman, one of her heroes, she remembered that those who forgot history would have to repeat it. She didn't mind. She had always loved her fellow creatures. And now that she found herself on the Earth planet she had become interested in Edgar Cayce, the seer who was so much like the one who comforted so many when he served the Creator and his fellow man in serving the Law of One.

She had written some of her story. It was in a modest magazine given over to spiritual matters, and in one page she was able to express what lessons she had learned in the fall of her former land—Atlantis. Not so distant as the Lord counts time and space. She addressed herself to what had gone amiss in that other place, now only a dream in so many hearts, and what she feared might be repeated again in the land she had learned to love as she had the other so long ago. Being well-read and well schooled, and sensitive to change, she had seen the warning signs where others older and more powerful than she had been blinded by an overabundance of good fortune. But it was never too late, even as the ship was leaving the dock and the planes were poised for the take-off. She saw the human frailties, the indifference to others and lack of gratitude to the Lord for the gift of life. Of which there was no greater gift. One thought kept running through her mind as she picked out books for the book lovers who came into her chambers, and that was saving the world. Yes, she, Verna, not yet thirty, unwed, but full of love for her brothers and sisters everywhere. Wanting to spread that love, especially on learning from the new prophet of these times that the Son of Man would be making His presence felt in a world waiting for the Millennium. Not knowing what it would bring.

She prayed this would be the world she would find.

"There is time for a worldwide healing to occur. We have it in our power to prevent destruction from taking place."

These words had come to her in the night. Many people, remembering that past, felt it was already too late to even try. But Verna disagreed. It was never too late to get to know your God. "Every time I wake up in the morning and hear a bird singing and every time I look into a beautiful blue sky, I feel hope in my heart. In spite of all our problems and suffering it is still a beautiful world."

She believed in the power of prayer, for she felt that little could be accomplished without it. She had read something about Atlanteans like herself moving off to Egypt after their land was destroyed by the crumbling of the earth and the wrath of the seas. She had read, too, all she could about Egypt and its connection with her homeland. She was intrigued by the pyramids, for she felt, despite their stony silence, that they were old enough and wise enough to harbor the secrets of the ancient past.

Like so many, she thought the pyramids had a message not only for God's children but also for the godless. She saw the tombs of the past as talismans of that past and symbols of the future. "Not only are they recognized as holy by the ancient Egyptians, the pyramids assuming the shape of the human body in meditation—legs criss-crossed, back straight, arms resting loosely on knees. Meditation—prayer—joining together the three sides—the physical, the spiritual and the pulsating earth. Each possessing the power to influence the others."

The pyramids, grim and forbidding, had a greater purpose than housing the mysteries of the past. Verna knew from Atlantis, as young as she was, that our lives belong to the present and future. The past did its part in connecting us to what lies ahead. She used symbols of the past to help not only herself but others sharing this life experience. For none of us, she knew, lived alone on an earth that was what we made of it with the approval of the Lord. She had read what a great American president had said in the midst of a struggle to preserve the Union. The precise words escaped her, but not the essence. "Without the Lord," he said, "we can do nothing."

The Union had been saved, its leader going on, His work done.

This was her country now. Atlantis was no more than a mirage at times. The memories dimmer as the present molded her mind, bringing her closer to the Law of One—the Law of the Lord—which never changed, whatever the time or place. For one place was so much like another, as the world became one. Both heaven and earth. Even unto the sun and moon

that ruled this small part of His Universe. There was no
end to the spirit the Lord had given her, which she
knew was immortal. It was like the wind, which blew
up a storm then became still, to return as the Lord
willed. As fresh and renewed as before.

The world never became so great she couldn't embrace it. For as she loved others she loved her Creator.
"For a meditation to heal the earth I fill my heart with
love and visualize a pyramid surrounding the earth,
cleansing it from all pollution, all fear, all suffering. I
imagine this pyramid sending healing energy to the
earth and to its inhabitants as I think of all the energy
centers in our land—East, West, North, South—and
those abroad in Europe, Asia, Africa and the Middle
East, where the Son once sojourned."

She saw the people absorbing the earth's vibrations
and pulsating with light. Influencing all sides of the
triangle, which represent the Holy Spirit—the Trinity
in man.

She wondered how God meant so many different
things to people, even in Atlantis, where some still believed while others joined with Belial like the spoiled
children they were. How else could she think of these
forbears, hoping they may have had their lesson and
mounted new lives, where the dimmed past was remembered only in His light.

For Verna, God was not harnessed to any specific
creed. He was everywhere. He belonged not to everyone but with everyone. A friend of Verna's wondered
how she could believe in God when she no longer went
to church. It was something to consider since so many

she knew were avid church-goers and lived by God's word. But for Verna God was universal. In the wind and the seas, in the skies and forests, in the hearts of man. And yes, the animals. For they, too, were His creations.

How could she answer this? With tact and diplomacy or the directness that had become part of her nature as her love for the Lord blossomed?

She responded as gently as she could and still say what was in her heart.

"I absolutely believe in God," she told her friend. "I just don't believe in the bureaucracies that exist in His name."

The friend was only partially appeased. "Well," she said, "you believe in your God, I'm sure."

Verna caught the sharpness in the other woman's voice.

"There is one God,'" she said evenly, "and no matter what we call ourselves, we can all be on different paths to Him."

The friend turned away. The answer had not satisfied her. Her God did not recognize any other God.

Verna thought about it. She was sophisticated enough to realize that God could be—and should be—all things to all people. And yet the denial of this was the cause of so much hostility and anger in the world. The last thing her God would want. She remembered Edgar Cayce saying that divisions over religion had been a factor in more confrontations and wars than anything. And now on the eve of the Millennium with so many expectant of Christ's resurrection, how could there be any divisions when all he counseled was that man should love and help each other.

It was not the religion that was wrong-minded, not the church, for that was only a mindless building, a place of worship to be sure, but no more sanctified than the beautiful skies and mountains the Lord had created. It was the people whose minds were closed to the hearts of those who felt differently. Nothing seemed to have changed in thousands of years.

"It is separatist thinking like hers," Verna thought, "that is the root of our world's problems today. We define each other by color, gender and occupation. Yet regardless of the differences, there is something inside us that is the same. That makes us all one. And that is God.

"If some of us were in Atlantis during the great upheavals and are now given another chance to heal ourselves and the earth, perhaps it is a blessing that we are not as technically advanced as we were in Atlantis."

She went on to quote a woman who had spoken much about the power of love.

"Author Marianne Williamson says that if we don't heed these warnings and mend our ways, our children will invent something much worse than the nuclear bomb. And sooner than this we may have to contend with the predicted pole shift."

Verna was not concerned about what havoc might be wrought by a polar shift, which last occurred tens of thousands of years ago according to some scientists. The shift, affecting the earth's magnetic field as said, had taken place 700,000 years ago and wasn't slated for a complete reversal for thousands of years.

As Verna knew so well, being an ardent believer in the wisdom of Edgar Cayce, a rise in the human consciousness, a renewal of faith in the brotherhood of man could blot out sunspots that affected the earth's magnetic field, with a resulting influence, adversely, on the earth's polar axis.

It was all very complex unless you were a scientist, and they only seemed to make it more complex, differing from each other even as the earth kept wobbling along on its axis, headed for whatever future the Universal Mind—the Creator—had in store for the children He had spawned.

Verna had no misgivings about the future. She fell back on what Edgar Cayce had said about a bright new Millennium emerging in a world where positive thoughts could affect the ruling sun and companion planets. While I wasn't that sure of this, I was sure that, despite all the scientists and scribes straining to get out their dire predictions, Cayce was correct in his assumption that the shifting of the pole would be a gradual process that even the gloomiest scientists would survive.

Verna saw the positive side.

"Edgar Cayce said that people of superior knowledge and abilities caused their own destruction by their greed for power and misuse of those abilities to intimidate and prey on those weaker than themselves. Thousands of years later we are fighting the same karmic battles and potentially face the same end that we did in Atlantis.

"I believe we have time to cancel our karmic debt and the ability to shift our perceptions. A shift of the material plans will not be necessary. It will take a lot of love and a lot of healing, starting with each of us. On a larger scale, many people are praying every day to raise their vibrations enough to spare us the severe lessons of Atlantis. If enough of us believe that this is possible and we work very hard together, we can truly unite to build a better place for those souls who will come after us.

"I plan to be here when wars will only be something to read about in history books, when people will have to look up words like *incest*, *gangs*, *terrorism*, and *prejudice*, because no one but a few aged people (like me by that time) will know what they mean. The souls that come after us will be unwilling to believe that we once viewed our brothers and sisters as different and separate from us simply because of their looks or beliefs. I dream of what life will be like in this future world that we do have the power to create. I hope to see you there.

"Edgar Cayce said that it is a privilege to incarnate and have another chance to live the right way. We must remember this and be mindful of our every word and thought. There will still be suffering and pain for some, but it is our duty to help them always. We might not be able to be there physically and we may not be able to donate our time or be able to afford monetary contributions, but we are always able and can always afford to send our love, to remember them in our prayers, and to send them healing light for their recovery."

It was a Utopian world that Verna Austen was visualizing, but it was no more than Edgar Cayce had foreshadowed with the Millennium if mankind chose to escape the lessons of a subcontinent that may have disappeared with the Biblical flood, leading to the dispersal of survivors to Egypt, Asia Minor, and the Caribbean area, namely Mexico, Central America and South America.

Verna had a number of regressions that took her back to her prehistoric home. They gave her greater insight into a present life, the only one Cayce says we could live now, and to her visions of the past. In her regressions, without Atlantis being mentioned, she saw beautiful shining towers, sparkling beaches with white sand and glittering palaces made entirely of crystal.

"I saw many white obelisks whose pyramid tops were made of crystals. It felt like Egypt but the land was much too lush and green. It could only be one place, Atlantis. I could hardly believe my eyes. My heart leaped at the sight of my ancient home. I longed to stay, but it wasn't to be."

The vision of Atlantis stayed and grew. She didn't talk about it. Not for fear of being ridiculed, but of a memory that was very private and painful. A memory of being molested as a child which had taken her to the hypotherapist's couch.

"I know," she said, "that many people of the New Age, with its sophisticated thinking, believe that we choose to be abused. That before we incarnate we know exactly what will happen to us in every lifetime and that by choosing such painful experiences we will advance faster spiritually.

"This," she emphasized, "is not true. We may know that we have a history with a certain soul and we may know things that have happened in past lives, but there is no rule that says it will happen again. Because we have free will we choose what we learn and what we teach. By choosing the role of a sex abuser, and then repeating it, the hardened abuser then tries to fill the emptiness he feels within with alcohol and drugs, and by hurting others. But there can never be enough of these escapes to fill the empty places inside of him, because only God can relieve these dark places."

The ordeal she had experienced, in a present reality and an Atlantis recollection, had turned her to a God she had communed with from childhood. He was very real, helping when no one else could have helped. "Only God can give us the peace we try to attain with food, money, alcohol and drugs. They are not the basic problems but plainly symptoms. Somehow we know we are not living up to our potential, fulfilling the mission God sent us here to accomplish. We have a part to play in healing the world, something that can only be done by us. Before we are able to do this, we must settle our unresolved issues from the past, whether from five years ago or five thousand years.

"We need to heal our past before we can create our future."

As a librarian she relates some of her present life to what she did in Atlantis:

"The Library and the Temple of One are similar places. Both occupations have to do with helping people find what they are looking for. They are both places that help to spread information. In whatever job we work at it is important to see the people with whom we come into contact as fellow human beings, fellow travelers on the path. It is a shame that we tend to see our lives in terms of events that we participate in—someone's wedding, a party, a new job—instead of really connecting on a soul level with each other. How many times do we really mean it when we ask someone how they are?

"When we view our lives as events instead of as moments that we have with each other, we fail to see the unlimited human potential that is within every one of us.

"Once I overheard a conversation between two people. One person said, 'Oh heck, it's Monday again, I hate Mondays.'

"The other replied, 'Isn't it great, I love every day.' I try to adopt this attitude. It doesn't really matter how the weather is, what time it is, what's going on this evening. What matters is that our lives are made up of perfect moments, unlimited opportunities to connect with each other's lives.

"That was the profession of those of us who worked in the Temple of One, people sharing their light with others. We can still do this today, in whatever job we have."

Verna had the nagging notion that she was not doing all she could do to help the world get in stride with the

Lord or heal the wounds of childhood. So she went to the therapist's couch again and turned up another episode in her Atlantean experience. She had known her sexual abuser then. She was one of the Keepers of the Way, the spiritual caretakers whose job it was to oversee the healing in the Temple of One. "We were also responsible for the Great Crystal and making sure it was only used to further our highest ideas. This immensely powerful crystal acted as a giant battery and combined with the rays of the sun could provide the energy transporting ships over the land and through the air, moving large objects and aiding in the construction of temples and great homes."

The possibilities, as she saw, were endless. Corresponding with Cayce's description of research leading up to the Death Ray, and with laser surgery and healings with beams of colored light.

She was chosen as the Head Keeper of the Temple eventually, overseeing other Keepers, one being the man who had abused her on the earth and in Atlantis. He was dead set against her and was forcibly removed. She sensed his hatred as he swore eternal revenge. With this came her realization that sexual abuse was not about sex at all, but about the theft of power, the desire—or lust—to control. For the first time she realized she had been trapped all her life in her own fears of molestation, of the torment of feeling soiled and impure.

"I thought and prayed long and hard for weeks. I no longer believed I had been born bad. I knew that somewhere inside me the tiny spark of God had enabled me to survive. I would no longer need to look outside myself—or God—for guidance. I would no longer trim my life to what others thought. I would no longer call myself a survivor, because it would imply I had been a victim. I was victimized, yes, but only I could call myself a victim. But no longer. Let others think as they would.

"I was inspired by the story of Anne Frank, who in spite of the misery and horrible oppression she experienced, was able to rise above her ordeal, to believe that people really are good at heart. Anne Frank in her concentration camp was able to see beyond the horrors and the pain and the fear to a place with God where we are all One.

"This was the law that the Children of the Law of One followed in Atlantis, before they were overcome by their false pride and idle thoughts of grandeur. Taking them from the One to whom they owed their everything. And then came the earthquakes and the storms, and the Flood. And then it was too late. A Keeper like myself had little authority with the Sons of Belial, the apostles of the devil, who ruled. But not for long. For God ruled differently.

"I well remember the time. Many of us Atlanteans now fear the storms and earthquakes and other aberrations of nature that preceded the Earth Changes. Some even have memories of the earth falling through the sky.

"Edgar Cayce tells us that the destruction of Atlantis in 28,000 B.C. coincided with the Biblical story of Noah and the flood.

"Noah, whose name in Aramaic means, One who will comfort the world, was truly a hero, a man who lived by his faith when all around him people were lost in despair. During the time in which he lived, the earth people did not live by God's law. Materialism and self-seeking concerns were the only laws of the land.

"God grew impatient waiting for people to change their ways. Eventually He decided to send a message that could not be ignored. 'Behold, I will bring a great flood of waters, and every living thing on earth shall die.' People were warned that the destruction could be averted, but they didn't listen. Then God commanded Noah, who honored the Lord, to build the Ark that he and his family would not die. His neighbors scoffed.

"The destruction of Atlantis was their own doing. In their quest to rule the world, they misused the tools they had invented for healing and spiritual knowledge, using them to exert control over all living things on earth. Edgar Cayce tells us that the final destruction came about when the Great Crystal, cared for so lovingly in the Temple of One and used only for the greatest good, was instead turned into a Death Ray, whose energies were pressed onto the earth as an atomiclike weapon. It was believed that these killing rays would travel through the earth and destroy everything in their path, thus establishing Atlantis's dominion on the earth.

"While this was happening, there was much preparation behind the scenes. The Children of the Law of One had been warned and were preparing the way for those who would come after them. They hid their records and traveled to distant lands to give warnings. They did not colonize these lands, but came instead from a love for all of humanity. They were forced to destroy what they could not transport, most notably the crystal skulls of Atlantis."

Verna recalled her stated role with the Keepers of the Way. "Because these crystal skulls were encoded with such power from the healings in which they were used, it became necessary to destroy most of them to keep them from falling into the hands of the Sons of Belial. Many refused, believing it was blasphemy. But gradually they saw that it was a test. Did we not know that the power to heal lies within? We used these crystals only as helpers, as symbols of our power. The few skulls that were saved were hidden. A time will come when they will be gathered up, signaling that the New Age has finally arrived.

"As the Atlanteans were given ample warning and time to prepare, so are we. It is not too late. We still can join our brother, whatever his country, whatever his skin color, whatever his name for God. We will finally see that we are more alike than we are different.

"The Children of the Law of One prepared the way for us, having the foresight to see there would come a time when all over the earth, people would need to stand hand-in-hand and call out the word.

"That word is, 'Brother.' "

Chapter Nine
The Seekers

Doug Richards was an amiable good-looking man. Looking more Hollywood than a professor. Bouncing around more like an athlete than an explorer looking for an island empire that had died ten thousand years ago. And being very *eloquent*.

"As far as I'm concerned, Atlantis is very real. I can picture it as Edgar Cayce visualized it in all its grandeur and then its fall. I can see where we have a lot to learn from what Cayce said. I'm not a professional geologist or oceanographer, which may be a help since I'm not married to any of the fixed concepts that have failed to turn up about Atlantis. There has been some evidence of its past, but nothing that's tangible. Not after thousands of years with all that shifting sediment on the floor of the ocean around the Bahamas. Edgar Cayce gave us the boundaries—and the spur—and we're shooting for the Millennium. The New Age."

He pondered for a moment. "Everybody wants the gold idol that proves they got Atlantis. Yet it seems to me that the search may be even more important than the discovery. For, more and more, in searching you get an idea there's some connection between us and them. They have a lot to tell us. To get wherever we're going, helps to know where we came from. The popular idea today is of gradual progress from a caveman with a club in his hand to our wonderful civilization. And that it can't help but get better. There are others who think it's all due for a big crash and we'll never recover. But looking at what Cayce said, you can see a cyclical sort of thing. Where the Atlanteans had a high culture, made some mistakes and crashed. We seem to be on the same edge now. Riding the crest, with lots of greed and lust for power. If we find the remnants of Atlantis, I think it could be the greatest thing in the world for the world, especially the people who laugh at the thought of a Lost Continent. For then we'll find a lot of people changing their tune and saying, 'We better get our act together or we're going to end up the same way.'"

I was somewhat more optimistic about this, having Cayce's assurance that the approaching Millennium was going to be essentially positive, apart from whether Atlantis was a myth or a harsh learning reality. Richards was saying what other explorers were saying. But I had a feeling it would take a lot of doing by people who thought like him to change the prevalent view that Atlantis was a myth.

He shook his head. "It's not a myth as long as we learn from the stories that have come down about them, beginning with Plato, then on to where Cayce made it all come alive. You have to ask yourself, if he was so right about so many things, why can't he be right about a Lost Continent, where he describes the people and the land with such vivid detail that you can just sense the overwhelming pride and selfishness that brought them down?"

He spoke with such vigor and enthusiasm that I asked, "What is personally driving you?"

"Well, I have a sense of the metaphysical, which brought me to the Cayce readings, having worked for a couple of years with Dr. Joseph B. Rhine, the psychic researcher, in his laboratory at Duke University. That opened the doors of consciousness for me, but it didn't have the excitement of getting out where the action was and grappling with reality.

"There's a sense of history. Something exciting to do, deep-diving, studying the geology as opposed to sitting in an office or lab. For the higher purpose there's a feeling of transforming things in terms of what our civilization thinks of itself. If you come on something tangible, something that could smack of Atlantis, people will take it and run with it. So ultimately there can be a greater awareness of our potential for destroying ourselves again or being constructive."

I had an idea the Cayce readings had a lot to do with getting him involved.

He nodded. "There's a Cayce reading where Cayce suggests that a committee could be set up to dig into all the stuff that had to do with his readings. He was that sure. There are lots of people working on it today because of him. Where there's anything that helps people address their spiritual side, Cayce says go for it. Looking for Atlantis isn't going to make any of us any money. Somebody may have a big Atlantis resort there on Bimini but it won't be me. A lot of the problems with the Atlantis research is that Cayce emphasized that you have to work like thunder, and with the exception of a handful of divers, almost everybody who's come down looking for Atlantis spends a week in Bimini, takes a few pictures, goes on a dive trip, takes a look at a few old rocks that look like paving stones, and then calls the *National Enquirer* and says they found Atlantis. What we need to get is some professional divers, go deeper, and then set up our paraphernalia on the edge of the Gulf Stream. The Gulf Stream current washes away the sediments, so you have bare rock to determine whether it's a natural formation or man-made, hopefully Atlantean. There are other good diving spots mentioned by Cayce, but they're hard to find in trackless water."

I thought of the effort going into all this searching for something that could very well be no more than a dream.

He had no trouble reading my mind. "It takes somebody with some maverick tendencies to be willing to do it. And you have to convince yourself that in the end you'll discover something that will benefit mankind. Your mind has to be open but not so open that your brains fall out. So far it all ends up in a lot of hard work. Then I fall back on the Cayce readings. And I realize that we in general, and me in particular, need that extra spiritual dimension in life to make sense of it. So what I got out of the Cayce readings was a sense of how to find the meaning of what we're doing. And keep feeling at one with everyone that's working at it like we are. I've seen a lot of people go off the deep end with Atlantis and do nasty things to each other. In fact, this is fairly standard. It's standard in archeology, and life in general. And that's where the Cayce spiritual measure helps. It would be nice to feel real good even if Atlantis wasn't there and either Cayce was wrong or we were wrong in the way we went about it. Meanwhile, we learned a lot about ourselves. And a lot of everything we were about. With all the reverses there's still a way to have some personal growth. Instead of what you so often see everywhere else, people so busy stabbing somebody in the back so they can get rich and famous. So that they lose track of why they're here in the first place. Except as examples of how so many got in the Atlantis Cayce visualized before its destruction.

"Cayce wasn't a prophet whose prophecies were written in stone. He frequently told people they could change what he saw with the free will God had given them. And discouraged them from living by whatever he told them—and not following their own soul. But not with Atlantis. He never changed his belief in the Atlantis he saw. For it was his way of warning people everywhere of dangers of our reliving the Atlantean experience. With the same disastrous result.

"He never joked about Atlantis as he did some predictions he dealt with. One man came to him, saying, 'Is the prediction true that I will die suddenly at the age of eighty in Tibet?' And Cayce would say, 'Well, if you live to be eighty and you visit Tibet, it's possible you'll die there.' "

Richards was still betting on Cayce. "He was right on target with his geology. When Cayce talked about where you could find significant things in the Bahamas, minerals and things, he said you have to go down to twelve- to fifteen-foot levels under the current Bimini surface. It turns out when they were dredging the channel, they dug up a piece of mangrove peat, organic material, nine feet below a surface that dated back nine thousand years. So with the twelve thousand years back that Cayce was talking about it was even deeper. So when you see the current island of Bimini, none of that was visible in the time frame Cayce gave. It was completely awash."

So if this was the Atlantis Cayce was talking about, it was rising as he said it would.

Richards was so dedicated I found myself hoping that he would come on Atlantis long before his hair and teeth fell out.

"Do you still have as strong a desire as when you started off so hopefully years ago?"

"Absolutely. Whatever I find or don't find, my

major driving force is still the same. To find where we came from and why we're here. When we find enough to know there was an Atlantis, then we can determine pretty well that everything else Cayce said about the island, with all its grandeur—and decay—was true."

I muddled over it a little.

"And so we find an Atlantis, how does that bring us closer to a solution of why and how we're now on an earth that Cayce says will be in pretty good shape for quite a time?"

His brow knit for a moment. "I don't know if it brings us closer in an easy way. You can't deny that things are very complex in terms of where we came from even when we find Atlantis. But you have many interpretations of what it means. My feeling is that at the point where we find something's really there, we're going to have all kinds of ideas about what we're about and what it means for our future." He smiled. "And whatever they are, if it gets everybody thinking, that's something in itself."

Richards had a partner in his search for the future. She was, improbably, a former high school principal with a passionate interest in the nature of God and man in the life experience we share.

If you were a Hollywood producer and casting for a movie, a middle-aged Joan Handley might be the last person you would choose to be the adventurer who put her conventional past behind her to begin a passionate search for a Lost Continent that has titillated the world's most venturesome explorers for centuries. She doesn't claim to be an expert. She leaves that to the geologists and underwater divers who have been navigating the waters around Bimini for decades without anything more exciting to show for it than a few paving stones and some mangrove peat.

She was challenged early on when a geologist who had never been on Bimini told her not to waste her time. All the stones the other geologists found were no more than beach rock. As they were scientists and she was a high school principal, she might as well stop right there.

Joan Handley laughed and decided that being a principal was a much more difficult job than being a geologist. Anyway, that kind of geologist. "From his easy chair he proclaimed."

She had the right qualities: endurance and perseverance. Being a high school principal in Miami could be demanding. But it was never dull. She was a disciplinarian when she had to be. For she liked effort, the kind of effort that was getting her entangled with the trials and mysteries of so many lost millenniums.

"As a school principal I didn't like to apply corporal punishment, although I confess that I did a few times. On my favorite kids, usually. As I saw they had a little more than some and could reach for their personal moons with some discipline and encouragement."

She had lost a child and that had caused her to reexamine her life and what she would do for the years ahead. "I really needed a passion to keep me going. My passion for my family was diverted into this search. I had been fascinated with the lost empire before I heard of Edgar Cayce. So many became involved by his descriptions of Atlantis.

"But with myself I think there was a built-in readiness for the search. It was a case of wanting to know where we were in the time frame so we could have an idea where we were going. That's the underlying thought. I've always been curious, even as a tiny girl, asking those 'why, why, why,' questions, and I really haven't got many answers, but I guess you just keep plugging away."

She looked up with a smile. "How about you? You've been writing your entire life. Haven't you been searching?"

"Well," I thought a moment, "my grandmother would always say God is everything and we kids would say, riveted by the eternal puzzle, 'Who put God there?' And she'd say, 'His will is Supreme.' I eventually decided He was always there. And that was why He was God."

With the new Millennium approaching, Handley, now a Cayce fan, has the feeling that Cayce's expectations of an Atlantis ultimately rising may be in sight. She believes that his predicted spiritual renaissance may yet be the most significant outcome of the tenacious search for an island empire that disappeared overnight—particularly since Cayce says its life could very well be a preview of our own.

As Handley points out, her search, like so many, goes beyond the physical dimensions of Atlantis or any other land.

"The end of the old age is coming," she says, "and

with the new Aquarian Age people are getting focused on the bettering of our society. I have the feeling we're right on schedule. It seems as though energy comes at the right time if we hold the ideal and monitor our motives."

She feels Atlantean searchers should have a sense of balance about what they're doing. She's seen people go haywire if they thought they found something like a man-made paving stone in deep water when it might have been a slab of beach rock, like the one her geologist adviser knew was beach rock before he saw it.

"It's more about tracing a civilization than it is about rocks and stones. Our quest appears so much more difficult than Egypt or South America [the Incas], but Atlantis was far grander than either of those ancient civilizations. The migrating Atlanteans, profiting by their own experience, didn't want their technological expertise to perpetuate itself. They wanted a clean start."

It was a little fanciful trying to impose the minds of a culture that may never have existed. But the Russians and other explorers have found enough on or near the mid-Atlantic ridge to indicate some subterranean land body—and there are millions everywhere clinging to the hope of an Atlantis that was a far better example for us before it disintegrated from a loss of spirit and defiance of the Lord.

The educator in Joan Handley was constantly peering behind the curtain of time for a deeper reason for a search taking so much of the searcher's energy and substance.

"*Our quest* is giving us something back. Something larger than money and attention. I think there's a lot of thought that the gritty problems the world is facing now are not going to be solved because people won't deal with it. This was something Cayce was saying right along. But if man is able to join in a global cause of survival, I believe that would prove that we have a greater potential for cooperation than we realize. Giving reality to the downfall of Atlantis, as Cayce has done, gives us some idea of what could happen to us. For as Atlantis became divided, with their people estranged, it was inevitable they would destroy themselves.

"I think more and more people will come to believe this is a possibility, that the cooperative society can get us into the future better than the competitive society that we have come to automatically believe in. We need more tolerance for each other, our religious beliefs, even our faults.

"With it all, even if Atlantis were a myth—which I don't believe—we have a lesson in survival here. A greater and more vivid example as the myth magically becomes reality through man's delving into his past."

Like other searches for man's identity, the Atlantean adventure plumbs deep into the hearts of people of every persuasion, nearly all with something very direct and intriguing in their outlook. And that is Mystery.

"I like the word *Mystery* attached to Atlantis," says Mark Thurston, a top psychologist and authority on the Cayce story. "The deepest sense of mystery, not just a

Sherlock Holmes kind of mystery but mystery with a capital *M*. For something in us knows, intuitively, there's got to be more to a story about human nature than the history books say. They speak so often of the activities of men, who with faith in the Creator can move mountains. So let us probe further.

"The fascination I have with Atlantis is that it reveals a human history that goes back farther than the typical history book says. It also says to me that human history isn't just a steady progress upward. It's like a roller coaster. We've had peaks and then valleys. When we realize that progress isn't always certain, because of free will, we see how we can make mistakes and send humanity into a tailspin. It puts much more responsibility back on us."

"You're saying 'we'?"

"The whole collective human family. When I first read about Atlantis, what was intriguing to me was this highly technological world that still had some connection with the spirit. There were these Children of the Law of One who still remembered their connection with the Creator. Then these other groups or souls, Sons of Belial. And with it there was a polarization of good and evil. Whereas in today's world, the distinction is often murky. It's harder to see what's helping or hurting humanity. Sometimes, even when it's obvious what helps and what hurts, there's still a gray area. In the Atlantis story it's very clear that some souls were committed to oneness and some to selfishness.

"In the 1930s and 1940s, with a worldwide depression and a worldwide war, it was very clear once again, with the villains pretty well defined, as they were in Atlantis, greed and the lust for power. In the nineties, approaching the Millennium, it's harder to get a handle on what's helping and hurting humanity. The Atlantis story states so graphically what Hugh Lynn Cayce, Edgar's son, used to say, emulating his father: 'With every deed and thought we're building up or tearing down.'

"The Atlantis story makes that point very clearly. The deeds are the fathers of the thought. I've been intrigued with how Cayce describes the Atlanteans as a thought people, given a psychic connection with their world. And more of a connection with the human family.

"What Cayce had to say about Atlantis had a snowball effect, more than some history books or earthquakes. I remember this one educator taking in the Cayce world affairs readings, with their allusions to Atlantis, and asking, 'What do those readings teach us about the twenty-first century? The Millennial century we're just a few hops and skips from. The conclusion was that unless we built a new world order based on Oneness, with the interconnection of all human life, we're going down the tube. But if we have this Oneness that Cayce spoke of, which Atlantis lacked, there's going to be a positive change."

I thought of the troublesome disharmonies in our society today. "Does that exclude differences and distinctions in race, religion, nationality, gender?"

"I don't think these distinctions are going to go away, but we'll be able to see beyond to the underlying oneness. I think there's still going to be different nations and languages." He laughed. "And different genders, I trust. But can we see through all that to the oneness?"

He thought of the violence of the day and the festering wars. "It isn't just the killing. It's millions of people sitting in front of the TV set in an alpha [higher consciousness] state concentrating on the news, enlarging its reality."

And so where does it all stop?

"You've mentioned that Cayce so often stressed that man, in a large sense, has the power to change his life and environment by his thought and spirituality."

Thurston nodded. "That's really what a prophet is supposed to do. He's supposed to give a warning and address what can be done to change things.

"Broadly speaking, I think we're hoping to find evidence that humanity has to rethink its future. If we rethink our past it makes sense that we're going to rethink our future. The principle that we tend to repeat our history suggests that once we open up and see our history in a different way, then we may see we've got to make some very important and difficult choices."

"If it's no more than a myth, it still may give new and positive dimensions to our lives. Without arguing whether Atlantis existed or not, or whether some of it is allegorical, it still gives some meaning to the human condition. It says things like we are responsible with our God-given free will with which we create our future. The Atlantis story, its rise and fall, emphasizes how just having great powers of the mind and of the spirit does not ensure our happiness.

"There's always the danger we may misuse those extraordinary expanded capabilities we are now expressing in communication. Which is why it's so relevant to this Millennium shift that we're moving into a realm where the powers of the mind are more and more evident. The Atlantis story is saying that the revelation of Atlantis could be a great boon for humanity, but only if we see the mistakes as well as the glory.

"But as Edgar Cayce said, we have a choice. We are, God willing, the masters of our destiny and, as the poet said, the captains of our fate."

Chapter Ten
God's Book

Edgar Cayce was a firm believer in the Bible. It was God's word through His prophets, and God didn't speak lightly, nor say anything He couldn't make good on. One of the Lord's statements that Cayce mentioned so often had something to do with a handful of God-loving people standing their ground against the hazards of life, whether they were the forces of evil or the furies of the elements.

One or ten men, said Cayce, from the Good Book, can make a difference if they hold on with faith in the Lord.

They didn't have to be a big hero like Lord Nelson or General Patton, but the so-called little man, humble and unsung, showing fortitude and leadership, as they dared the smoking volcano with the Aztec name of Popocatepetl—fondly known as Popo—from doing his worst.

Old Popo, some eighteen thousand feet tall, does its erupting in the heart of Mexico, some fifty miles from the throbbing metropolis of Mexico City, which looks over its shoulder from time to time to make sure Old Smokey (Popo) is still behaving. Our friendly neighbor to the south has had a few bad shots recently with El Niño blasting the resort city of Acapulco, causing a tragic loss of life and property. The nearby tragedy of their countrymen has left the people dwelling at the base of the volcanic mountain sympathetic but unafraid as they go about their daily routine of tilling their fields in and around the village of San Pedro, sending their children to church, praying to God and their patron saint, Don Gregorio, who some feel lives in Old Popo and will give them a signal when it is time to move on.

Meanwhile, the bravest are building new homes at the foot of the mountain, without any sign of fear, ignoring the acrid atmosphere. They have the feeling that the Lord and their favorite saint will not let them down. They pray every day to the Lord, to Jesus, and to Don Gregorio, who they feel is one of them. There are all kinds of official evacuation programs, but the villagers of San Pedro aren't interested. They've stood up to Old Popo for twelve hundred years, the last time it erupted. They hear now that it's time again, with another Millennial approach. But meanwhile they're sending out their positive vibes. As trouble brews else-where.

While the fabled island empire of Atlantis was grab-bing major attention as the Millennium approached, the infinitely smaller island of Krakotoa in the Indone-sian seas was giving us new insight into what may have happened to Atlantis in a series of volcanic ex-plosions eons ago.

Krakatoa was back in the news again, more than a hundred years after it was blasted off the map in 1883 in what at the time was the most powerful explosion ever recorded on Planet Earth. Three-quarters of the is-land disappeared in a roar that was heard around the world, shaking the island of Madagascar in the Indian Ocean. Thunderous 120-foot tidal waves stirred up by the blast killed almost forty thousand people in the coastal towns of Java and Sumatra. Huge tsunamis swept over the beaches of Hawaii and South America. And inundated the Philippines.

There had never been anything on earth like it be-fore. Buildings were shaken three thousand miles away. Tremendous explosions reverberated two thou-sand miles away in Australia. The skies for millions of people were obscured by clouds of ash and gritty smoke rising fifty miles to block the sun, while masses of pumice—porous volcanic rock—stopped seagoing vessels in their tracks. For many it seemed like the end of the world. Plant and animal life within hundreds of miles were affected for years. Continuing eruptions made themselves felt. There were panics throughout the world, amid talk of mankind facing extermination for its sins. Talk heard even today among the self-righteous doomsayers, saying Armageddon has arrived with a rumbling Krakatoa ready to blow up again, this time taking our world with it.

Detached observers saw comforting signs. Small eruptions continuing off and on formed a new island only a few miles from where the greater part of Krakatoa used to be. Some saw retributive significance in this rebirth of an island that had been given up for dead. The new island a few miles from the old was named Anak Krakatoa—the Child of Krakatoa.

It was heartening as the Millennium approached to watch a train of human beings climbing the Krakatoa slopes in search of adventure and the past. It was no Atlantis but it expressed the faith and resolve of man to learn from that past.

With the new Millennium on the horizon, many of an optimistic turn viewed the revival of the islands, still active, as indicative of the promised Resurrection.

As recently as 1996, new eruptions of a gentler nature were occurring on Krakatoa, plumes of dark smoke reaching for the sky. The offspring, Anak Krakatoa, was making itself felt, too. Doing very well for a baby. With its cinder cone forming in a few weeks and going into action.

"When you look at what remains of Krakatoa—or what it was," a geologist noted, "you have to wonder how anyone got out of Atlantis."

Currently the island authorities invite people from all over to visit Krakatoa's slopes and tread on the ground formed by molten lava thrown up from the fiery crater.

It was the same courage, and inspired faith in the Lord, that motivated these simple people to hang on when sophisticated city-dwellers would have been scooting for the nearest ferry.

Cayce put an erupting Pele on his active list for the New Age. The Hawaiian islands, namely its Kilauea Volcano, was known to homeowners as Madam Pele, the volcano goddess. Beginning in 1990 to give up a steady stream of lava ringed with fire consuming all the homes on its path to the sea.

Cayce warned of Pele's arrival in a pre-Millennial period ending in 1998. But as he pointed out many times, any disaster could be changed as man harbored thoughts of others besides himself. He evidently felt this spiritual change would take place by the Millennium, for he predicted later, despite all the prophecies of doom, a quiet period of gradual change in the earth's nature with a heightened One World consciousness.

Old Popo seems more representative of a changing Millennium, possibly because we have some evidence of its past in its present. There are heroes on every doorstep. People who saw no reason for leaving their homesteads because they felt protected by their God and His saint, Don Gregorio. I can't say too much for them. They are hard and tough, honest. They keep their morale high with the deep communal feeling that often develops in a small town that ekes its living out of the soil, bringing them closer to nature—and the Creator.

They have leaders who thought first of the others,

lifelong neighbors, and then themselves. One of these heroes, the hardy, outspoken Jaime Romero, dusting volcanic ashes from his face, was approached as he labored with some workmen on his new concrete-reinforced home at the base of the volcanic mountain.

"Why all this building with a smoking Popo liable to blow its stack at any moment?" he was asked.

"An investment in the future," Jaime Romero responded with a smile.

The kind of faith that moves mountains, according to Cayce. But, hopefully, not for another Millennium, thanks to the sublime confidence of a humble and spiritual people in God Almighty and his ambassador, Don Gregorio, who, some thought, would help the Millennium come in.

In his lifetime Edgar Cayce paid little attention to the doomsday prophets currently making headlines. Somehow the American public seemed more partial to mindless warnings of its own annihilation than Cayce's reassuring forecast—with God's word that the Millennial beginning will not be a hotbed of devastation, but the recycling of a spiritual age with a growing consciousness of brotherhood despite the false prophets Christ warned about.

Cayce saw the Aquarian Age beginning in the present year, 1998, when he expected his own presence to be felt. Apparently referring to the upsurge in portrayals of his life in film, books, and symposiums. He was asked what the New Age would mean to mankind in its emphasis on the mental and the spiritual. And he replied:

"In the outgoing Piscean Age, we had the entrance of God among men, with the birth on earth of the Christ. In this age there was the consciousness of the ability to communicate with the Creative Forces and the uses of same in a material way. This awareness in the age of Atlantis brought the destruction of man through selfishness, and the beginning of his journey upwards."

Cayce was optimistic about the survival of god's world as he knew it. In his portrayal of the Millennium change, he constantly saw a reassuring rise in spiritual values in America. As an inveterate Bible reader, he was familiar with the biblical prophets and their foreshadowing of the planet earth. He was drawn to the Books of Daniel, Ezekiel, Isaiah (the Prophet of the Coming) and Jeremiah, as well as Matthew and Revelation out of the New Testament.

Nowhere in these passages, he saw, was there any clear-cut prophecy of the end of the world, only an end of the beginning, with the regeneration of man, and a God ready to forgive those fallen by the wayside after repenting their sins in their rejection of the Ten Commandments.

Cayce was quick to assure any of the worried worldenders that the Millennium would slip in on little cat feet: "Concern yourself with the world inside you. And you will have little to concern you in the world outside you."

I have heard of the heralded end of the world, from evangelists preying on the fears of so many told that the earth will go the way of Atlantis—even as they thought Atlantis a myth.

There were many doomsdays. The world has been "ending" almost since it began. In a more rustic America, the Millerites, predecessors of the Adventists, gave away their earthly possessions, donned their ascension robes, and waited ecstatically for the world to stop. It didn't. And the founding father, William Miller, blaming a biblical miscalculation, braced his followers for a second assault on heaven. He died shortly thereafter, a disillusioned and broken man. The world had ended for him. But not for his disenfranchised followers. They started suing for the worldly goods they had given away in a burst of celestial emotion.

Every worldwide crisis, every great war, appeared to flush out a flood of biblical interpretations foretelling the end of times. The restoration of Israel as a nation, mirrored by the struggle between good and evil at Armageddon, served to quicken this feeling. But Revelation, as Cayce saw, did not presage the end. Not in this Millennium or the next. Cayce did see continuing trouble in the Middle East with Revelation's Babylon the Great, the Mother of Harlots and Abominations of the Earth. A timely forecast, since Babylon was the historic seat of Iraq's ruler Saddam Hussein, an avowed enemy of freedom-loving democratic nations. His capital, Baghdad, was usually associated with Babylon, in a region that later became Iraq.

Like the prophet Jeremiah, Cayce saw sporadic warfare in the Middle East, though Israel was not recognized as a nation until 1948, long before Saddam

Hussein became the most powerful leader in the Arab world. A constant thorn in the side of the Western world, first with his incursion into Kuwait, then subsequent defiance about the arsenal of secret weapons he had been building up since his defeat in the Gulf War.

The Iraqi president was likened by others, and by himself as well, to Nebuchadnezzar, the Babylonian king who destroyed Jerusalem five hundred years before Christ. Saddam speaks of the Mother of Battles, just as the Mother of Nations are spoken of in the Bible. But he overlooked in his comparison to an earlier rule of Babylon that Nebuchadnezzar was destroyed by God's will because of his forays against the Israelis of that time.

Cayce, a lover of the Bible, would have been intrigued by the passages in Jeremiah dealing with the Lord's wrath with the ruler of Babylon, which, boasted Saddam Hussein, was no other than he.

Accordingly, in the Book of Jeremiah the Lord said:

Therefore hear ye the counsel of the Lord, that he hath taken against Babylon and his purposes. Surely the least of the flock shall draw them out. At the noise of the taking of Babylon the earth is moved, and the cry is heard among the nations. For Israel hath not been forsaken, nor Judah of his God, of the Lord of Hosts. Though their land was filled with sin against the Holy One of Israel.

We would have healed Babylon, but she is not healed. Forsake her, and let us go every one into his own country. For her judgment reacheth into heaven and lifted up even to the skies.

Her captains and her rulers, and her mighty men, they shall sleep a perpetual sleep, and not wake, saith the King, whose name is the Lord of Hosts.

The broad walls of Babylon shall be utterly broken and her gates burned with fire, and the people shall labor in vain, and the folk in the fire, and they shall be weary. Thus shall Babylon sink and shall not rise from the evil that I will bring unto her.

Cayce made no such predictions himself. They seemed superfluous. Back a lifetime ago Cayce was asked about the significance of the year 1998. As he did so often he said it would be a period of gradual change, with man beginning to realize his potential on a number of fronts, scientific as well as scriptural. He was obviously seeking to dispel the fears cast by the doomsayers. Downplaying any great turmoil for the Millennium, he said:

"In 1998 we may find a great deal of the activities as have been wrought by the gradual changes that are coming about. These are at the periods when the cycle of the solar activity, the years related to the sun's passage through the various spheres of activity are pertinent to the change between the Piscean and the Aquarian age. This is a gradual not a cataclysmic activity in the experience of the earth in this period."

In Revelation, in a reference to Armageddon, the ultimate battleground between good and evil, Cayce saw a positive victory for the forces of good, with an awakening in the New Age of the best elements in people, amid a peaceful revolution that will find jaded, self-serving rulers replaced by crusading leaders from the ranks of the people. He elaborated:

"As to those things that deal with the mental of the earth, these shall call upon the mountains to cover many. As ye have seen those in lowly places raised to those in power in the political, in the machinery of the nations' activities, so shall ye see those high places reduced and calling on the waters of darkness to cover them. And those that in the inmost recesses of themselves awaken to the spiritual truths that are to be given, and those places that have acted in the capacity of teachers among men, the rottenness of those that have ministered in places will be brought to light and turmoils and strifes shall enter. And as there is the wavering of those that would enter as emissaries, as teachers, from the throne of life, the throne of immortality, and wage war in the air with those of darkness, then know ye the Armageddon is at hand. For with the great numbers of the gathering of the hosts of those that have hindered and would make for man and his weaknesses stumbling blocks, they shall wage war with the spirits of light that come into the earth for this awakening, that have been and are being called by those of the sons of men into the service of the living God. For He, as ye have been told, is not the God of the dead, not the God of those that have forsaken Him, but those that love His coming, that love his associa-

tion among men—the God of the living, the God of
life. For He is life."

For America specifically, Cayce had a premonition
of the spiritual awakening that would be influenced by
John Peniel, blessed by [El-God], named in Genesis,
who he may have seen as the resurrected Christ reborn
with the renovation of the Millennium. He slips in the
stunning revelation under the guise of a question.
"Who," he asks, "shall proclaim the acceptable years
of the Lord in him that has been born in the earth in
America? Those from that land where there has been
the regeneration, not only of the body but the mind and
the spirit of men. They shall come and declare that
John Peniel is giving to the world the new order of
things. Not these that have been proclaimed and have
been refused, but that they are made plain in the minds
of men, that they may know the truth and the truth, the
light, will make them free."

It seemed inconceivable that such a revelation could
have been made by any prophet, particularly so devout
a Christian as Cayce, without some preface that would
break such earthshaking news. "I have declared this,"
said Cayce, "that has been delivered unto me to give to
you that sit here and that hear and see a light breaking
in the East, and have heard, have seen thine weaknesses and thine fault findings, and know that He will
make thy paths straight if ye will but live that ye know
this day—then may the next step, the next word, be declared unto thee. For ye in your weakness have known
the way through that which ye have made manifest if
the Spirit of the truth and light that has been pro-

claimed into this earth, that has been committed into the keeping of Him that made of Himself no estate but who brought into being all that ye see manifest in the earth, and has declared this message unto thee: Love the Lord thy God with all thy heart. And the second is like unto it, 'Love thy neighbor as thyself.' Who is thine neighbor? Him that ye may aid in whatsoever way that he, thy neighbor, thy brother, has been troubled. Help him to stand on his own feet. For such may only know the acceptable way. The weakling, the unsteady, must enter into the crucible and become as naught, even as He, that they may know the way."

As Cayce prophesied increasingly with the Millennium, communication would be quickened to the point where people in the other side of the world would be as accessible (except for bodily contact) as the next-door neighbor. The laser beams geared to carry messages and pictures around the world with the speed of light.

Cayce was constantly asked where and when the Messiah of the Millennium would reappear, indicating a growing rise of spirituality in the hearts of the American people. He was always encouraging, for he envisioned in dreams the Master's presence as the connecting link between peace and war, with the decisive force no longer the Holy Land:

"These then are those conditions as may be expected: The spirituality of the American people will be rather as a criterion of that which is to become the world's forces, for as has been [to Cayce] in that of the peace table, there sat the Master in the American people, with the brotherhood of the world accepted. War was at an end. Without same there will again come the Armageddon. And in the same there will be seen that the Christian forces will again move westward."

With America the new center of spirituality, as long as it pursued the tenets laid down by Christ and the Lord.

Chapter Eleven
The Aquarian Age

"What will the Aquarian Age mean to mankind as regards physical, mental and spiritual development?"

"You think this can be answered in one word?" asked Edgar Cayce. After a slight pause he added: "These are as growing pains, from the Piscean Age. In the center of same the Aquarian had the entrance of Emmanuel [the Christ] or God among men. Now with the Aquarian we have the full consciousness of the ability to communicate with or to be aware of the relationships to the creative forces and uses of same. This awareness, misused during the era in Atlantis, brought destruction to man because of his selfishness."

The answer was not what this thirty-nine-year-old

man was seeking, to heal his pain over the tragic end
of a young woman he adored.

Was he being selfish? He didn't think so. He had
lost his soulmate and life was empty without her. And
what of this Aquarian Age, with all its promise of a
great life and happy days? Somewhat disgruntled, he
asked, "Why is the Aquarian Age described as the Age
of the Lily?"

"Purity. The purity it represents in man will comprehend the awareness that belongs to those who seek
the way."

It was not time for him to understand. But what
Cayce was saying was becoming plain. What of the
young woman who had left? Was he thinking of her, or
only himself?

The Aquarian Age was an age of expectation, of
hope and revolution, of inventiveness, creation and
new life for those who were at one with the Lord. This
was the age of the beginning, the new and fuller life,
not necessarily confined in this solar system.

The man was confused. "How could anyone so
young, so beautiful, so loved choose to die?"

"Death is but a passing in and a passing out," Cayce
said. "For these are not the activities of individuals
who look on the earth as the center of its activities, but
of the soul. For that which caused the separation of
souls from the universal consciousness came not in the
sphere of materiality, but in that of spirit."

This increased awareness, said Cayce, was all part
of the new Aquarian Age, casting its *first* shadow in the
year 1975. "In that age the new race is coming. The

children belonging to that generation will be very inquisitive. And very bright. Brighter than their parents."

I had noticed that the children of that period seemed to be more sensitive and alert than some born in previous generations. But I put this down to home television, which gave youngsters a greater awareness, and the use of computers, which a twelve-year-old child seemed to manage better than myself.

Cayce had some original notions of his own on that score. "Now why is it that people feared God all these centuries and now they don't? Suppose you have a son three or four years old. He isn't afraid of anything. When he grows up, say eight years old to about fourteen years old, he is taught to obey for fear of punishment. When the children are eighteen years of age they don't fear their parents. They begin to love them. They are grown up at eighteen. The next generation will be grown up at twenty-one, in the light of spiritual evolution.

"The fear of God, just waiting to catch you or punish you, appeals to the child mind. Do not fear God but love God. Do not fear death, but conscience. The next generation will be coming on earth and will not be fooled when the Aquarian Age fully arrives in 1998, as a tune-up for the Millennium. It will be a matter-of-fact generation. It will not believe in blind faith, but in scientific facts and demand a new religion of love and freedom from dogmas and misconceptions."

Looking ahead to the Millennium, Cayce saw more Aquarian influence in the people he counseled than any other astrological sign: three thousand Aquarian aspects in the fourteen thousand readings he gave. For the most part he saw Aquarians as strong-minded, resourceful, interested in people. They were the greatest of crusaders. He spoke often of President Franklin Roosevelt taking a tight hold on the country, bringing his New Deal to the common man. He saw the Aquarius leaders fashioning the New Age as a manifestation of their sign, so often spearheading the revolutions characteristic of Aquarius with force and social reforms that helped create and shape a new kind of world.

All one has to do is look at the nation's history, beginning with George Washington: Calendar revisions of his birth reveal him as Aquarian rather that Pisces. As for Lincoln, Cayce frequently mentioned him as the greatest Aquarian of all, with a strength and kindness, a humility and reverence for the Lord, almost Christlike—a leader, who like Christ, Cayce pointed out, was "crucified" with an assassin's bullet for what he did to free the slaves and bind the nation's wounds.

Cayce thought of all this as he was reading for an Aquarian in a family crisis, someone he saw had the "strength, harmony and understanding" where many another might break. In his unconscious state, he saw that she had the strength and purpose to control the pressing problems confronting her, and the wisdom:

"As to the influences that arise from the astrological sojourns, these are rather in keeping with the time. The Aquarian forces, and as there are the beginnings of the Aquarian age."

The reading was unusual, for he was looking

decades ahead, though, as he said, the Aquarian Age took years maturing before its advent in 1998. In encouraging a younger woman, an Aquarian, he said, realizing her strengths, "Do not consider self as being unusual because unusual experiences arise in thy associations, in thy meditations, in thy activities with thy fellow man. Do not do other than contemplate." He paused, hesitated a moment, then delivered his shocker:

"Remember thou art in the same signs, omens, as the Mother of Him that gave to the earth the physical man, Jesus—Aquarius in its perception—perfection."

The woman sat still for a moment, hearing her own breathing. Unable to speak. Cayce went on: "When those experiences arose in that life, it was said, 'She pondered these in her heart.'

"Hence the same injunction might be given today. For no better direction can be had or given than the consecrating of self in body, in mind, in activity to the service of that influence, those forces that the self may give to others in the meditations, the supplications, keeping self in those directions that indeed are as He gave: 'Ye abide in me, I in the Father,' and ye may know those forces from the abiding presence of the Master."

I wonder how Cayce had known that Mary, the mother of Christ, was an Aquarian. The world knew Jesus as a Capricorn, but many felt he was the perfect Aquarian, embracing the world. And that the ancients were mistaken on his birthday, December 25 being the established date. February 6, the date of a special constellation, was the choice of some astronomers, who related the latter date to the Three Magi—three astrologers—who had followed the course of Jesus' star to Bethlehem.

Cayce soon indicated how the Holy Mother's birthday was known to the woman he was advising some two thousand years after the event:

"The entity," he said, "was among those, or that one that would be termed as the waiting maid with Elizabeth [mother of John the Baptist] and with Mary when each were heavy with child. At their meeting when there was the awareness of that as was to come to the pass, the entity then was that one that blessed them both, and made those prophecies as what would be the material experience of each in the earth.

"Then in the name Anna, the entity waited in the preparations for the maidens who consecrated their love for this expectancy in those periods. Hence the entity was then known as a seeress, a prophetess, and is one in the present that may find innate experiences coming through voices, through sounds as of music, through the rushing of mighty winds. But know, my child, their source when such things come to pass."

It would have been good to be present when the young woman with Cayce heard of her past. It must have come like a thunderbolt that she should have been that close, past life or not to the figures she had revered from childhood.

That past in her thinking, and her Aquarian nature, now dictated the activities that made her of help to others, giving her the strength to deal with her own problems brought on by her youth and beauty.

"Those activities," said Cayce, "will enable the entity to counsel those who seek to know the experiences of every nature pertaining to a soul movement or activity. Hold not to things of the flesh or of the earth, but to that as thou didst give in assisting not only those mothers but the young women, the maidens of that blessed day. For thy counsel gave strength to many. Abide ye in that strength that may keep thee first, and may aid thee in counseling others."

Cayce saw that the young woman had such concern for the purification of her body that it was almost an obsession in the present. "These are well," he enjoined, "but remember those forces as He gave. That which cometh from the body, not that which goeth in defileth same. That which is the expression of thy relationships, keep. For not faith alone but works of faith make for the proper purifying, the proper concentrating, the proper relationships."

She was brimming with questions, as who wouldn't be. But none dealt with her service with the two famous cousins—Mary and Elizabeth. Instead she referred to the prospects of her current life: "Have I any healing power? If so, how may I develop it?"

"By raising those vibrations within self to the consciousness of the Christ force, and giving it out through the hands and through the thoughts."

The next question showed more of her dedication, possibly springing out of a hazy past. "For what did I come into this plane at this time?"

Cayce saw in this life a continuation of the preparation of the past, though not as mind-boggling. "To be the aid, the help, to many that are seeking their way through the earth's experience at this time. Not for self, then, but others, that their strength might be increased. That thy own glory and power may be the stronger in Him. Hold fast to that trust in Him as ye read the Fourteenth Chapter of Saint John, as ye read in Luke thy blessings in the temple, there will be given thee much that is beyond words here."

This was not an ordinary reading. I understood that he pored over it long, with gratitude in his heart for the privilege of having touched on the lives of those close to the heart of the Master he venerated.

The Aquarian Age was very special to Cayce. He saw the hope of the world brimming out of the rise of spirituality he foresaw with the dawning of the Millennium. He equated spirituality with oneness with the Lord, the Creator, the essence for our being.

As he saw the Aquarian Age, "It was an evolution in part of the development of the whole Universe, not just this consciousness of our own solar system. But of all solar force, of which our system is only a mere part of the whole consciousness. But in the earth and man's awareness of the three-dimensional consciousness, only those that have known same may leave same through the awareness of there being those influences through their various spheres of activity, including not only the earthly sojourns. but the sojourns throughout the spheres of activity when they are absent from a physical consciousness."

He was asked whether he was speaking about his rebirth.

He replied. "What does the *Word* say (meaning Christ's speaking of everlasting life)? He has not willed that any soul shall perish but has with each temptation, with each condition that has risen within the experience of the soul, prepared a way. These being a constant change being wrought. Not that through activities, but it is ever as the voice of the individual. It is that which creates the godly force within an individual, or a soul that makes it seek its level. He, the way, the Son, showed in materiality, the ability to become one with the Creative Forces as to pronounce his atonement with the Father-God. And so may all men, as He gave."

Some of the talk about the Aquarian Age was cryptic, but Cayce's replies were nearly always open and the same: that whatever proceeded out of the mouth or energy of man should be constructive.

He was asked, "Is it gradually becoming possible through the restoration of Phosphorous that man will talk back and forth with the Cosmos [the heavens]— like the radio principle?" Phosphorous, in Greek biblical times, stood for light or illumination, or in modern context the humble match head, which people often strike when they are in darkness and need light. "What," the man pursued, "does the restoration of Phosphorous signify?"

Familiar with the expression, in his subconscious state, Cayce quickly applied it to the Aquarian Age with its emphasis on universal awareness:

"The relationship of the individual to that awareness of the universal consciousness should be the promise of all who put their faith in Him. For as He has given, 'He that abideth in me and I in him, to him will be made aware of all things. This is all there in his words, in His promises to man. Just as indicated in his exhortation upon the activities of John [the apostle] as to what they meant in the affairs of man. And yet when individuals, even as John, become aware of being within the presence of life itself, God Himself made manifest how few accepted it.

"Only those who accept same will become aware of what's going on about them. How few realize the vibratory forces as great influences from even one individual to another when they are in the same vibratory force or influence. And yet ye ask what will the Aquarian Age bring in mind, body, experience."

Cayce had more to say about the restoration of Phosphorous. "It is interesting to note that *Phos* is a Greek word meaning 'light.' The word is used in the New Testament as in John. In Him was light, life, and the life was the light of men. And the light shineth in the darkness, and the darkness comprehended it not."

He had dug deep into his inner self. He sighed and said, "I am through."

UFOs (Unidentified Flying Objects) were very much a conceptual part of Edgar Cayce's vision of the Aquarian Age. Flying was something man had wanted to do since the beginning of time, and now it was being done, with or without man. Many people came to him troubled by some unexplained craft they had seen in the skies, usually at night, and he listened closely in his sleep, for he had some experience with them himself.

"One night, some weeks ago," this man was saying a little sheepishly, "I saw floating above my head in space an exceedingly bright sphere or planet. It seemed to be moving within itself as well as through space. Please interpret this for me, if you will."

Nothing surprised Cayce. He saw immediately it was not a shooting star, an airplane, or a figment of the man's imagination. It was, he said, without thinking what a shock it might be, a visitation from another planet on an exploratory journey from a lesser planet.

"As given," he said, "these individuals are reaching that period, that place in their experience, where the consciousness becomes more and more aware of the very lessons and truths being given out to manifest in the experience of selves and others. So, in the vision seen, it is the world without and the world within, the consciousness within self becomes more and more aware. Their movements as one coordinating with the other, the brightness of the orb itself that makes for the light, the understanding, the enlightenment that is obtained from within. Well was it said by Him, 'Ye do not light a lamp to put it out under a bushel.' "

Cayce saw the light as a good omen, whether a UFO or a shooting star. "When there is that consciousness within of being more and more in accord with the light that shineth even unto the darkness, though there may come strifes, though there may come disappointments, though there may come turmoils from without and within, yet His peace maketh for harmony, with that cooperation of the personality, the individuality, of self and thy God."

How, the man inquired, could he bring himself closer to the Lord? He was sorely troubled, and the light, he feared, may have been a warning, given that it could have been the message of a UFO.

Cayce was reassuring. He had seen flying saucers himself, without seeing anything ominous in them. Well aware of the limitless planets in God's universe, he thought it flattering that they may have had some interest in humble man, who knew so little of his origin or where he was going.

"Let that light that shines without be lighted by that light which is created from within, making the activities of the inner self and the outer self in accord, or let that seen of others be impelled by the light from the love of the Giver of life, light, and immortality."

The man was still troubled. "Is there no other way given among men whereby they may be saved?"

"Saved from what? Only from themselves. That is their individual hell. They dig it with their own desires. Look to yourself and the God within you. His light will shine brighter than any light to be seen in the sky."

Flying saucers, or UFOs, glimpsed in the night sky, had no mystery for Cayce. In reading for a man he saw as an Atlantean, he spoke of a life in another land where the "manners of transportation, the manners of communications through the airships of that period were such as Ezekiel described at a much later date."

The description in the Old Testament's Book of the Prophet Ezekiel was something even a casual reader of the Bible was struck by. It was picturesque and graphic. His planes had wheels and wings, cabins, and pilots who maneuvered the craft with the skill of modern aviators. The prophet's portrayal was chilling. For if he could be so explicit some thousands of years ago, the end of times predicted by the prophet Daniel may have long come and gone. The airport must have been an unusual one to harbor all the planes and the array of pilots. Ezekiel was a great reporter, missing little in the nature of detail:

"And when the living creatures [the pilots] went, the wheels went by them. And when the living creatures were lifted up from the earth the wheels were lifted up.

"Whithersoever the spirit was to go, they went. And the wheels were lifted up over against them for the spirit of the living creature was in the wheels.

"And the likeness of the firmament upon the heads of the living creature was as the color of the terrible crystal, stretched forth over their heads above.

"And under the firmament were their wings straight, the one toward the other. Everyone had two, which covered on this side, and every one had two, which covered on that side, their bodies.

"And when they went, I heard the noise of their wings, like the noise of great waters, as the voice of the Almighty, the voice of speech, as the noise of an host. When they stood they let down their wings.

"And there was a voice from the firmament that was over their heads, when they stood, and had let down their wings. As the appearance of the rainbow that is in the clouds in the day of rain, so was the appearance of

the brightness round about. This was the appearance of
the likeness of the glory of the Lord. And when I saw
it I fell upon my face, and I heard a voice of one that
spoke unto me."

I marveled at the eloquence of the prophet. Or was
this another episode in the never-ending recycling of a
world that has no beginning and no end. One man had
the answer. Edgar Cayce—the Sleeping Prophet.

Chapter Twelve
God the Astrologer

With the Millennium coming around, swarms of psychics and astrologers are making all kinds of predictions of Millennial disasters. They see wars in the Middle East, the Balkans, Africa, Tibet—wherever wars rage over slips of land and religious or racial differences. Edgar Cayce's voice is now silent, but his words live on. Yes, there would be wars here and there, he saw, but the United Nations, led by the United States, would put the quietus on the still prevailing threat, the Iraqi leader Saddam Hussein, continuing the struggle that former President Bush left unfinished. There would be trouble in Asia, with China continuing to flex its muscles. And this would be resolved.

There would be the mystical presence Cayce had

talked about, with people everywhere saying they had experienced a visitation from Jesus, whereas Cayce visualized Christ's Millennial manifestation in the hearts of people who crossed racial and religious lines to glorify His brotherhood.

Some of the flavor of biblical times would be restored as astrology, flourishing in Moses' time, would be revived in a new epoch where whole peoples would banish hatred and hostility from their hearts, even to a resolution of the end of the festival of hate between people of the same race in Ireland. And then wondering people could say with some justification that the Sleeping Prophet was right—at least figuratively—when he said that Christ would be striding into a new and better Millennium.

Cayce savored the days of the ancient prophets, who made warnings of their prophecies, so much as he did. For didn't the Old Testament, the Bible of Isaiah and Elijah, say that the mighty Philistine warrior Sisera struggled mightily against the stars to no avail? His death foreshadowed by the planets.

Cayce was no astrology buff. He didn't conduct his psychic readings with astrology charts at his elbows. Yet he wouldn't have been the psychic he was if he didn't realize that the cosmic rays impact that speck of earth known quaintly as the World. He didn't have to read the astronomers Kepler or Copernicus or Einstein, to know that we were in an infinite Universe of many solar systems, subject to the laws of the Creator who put us here. As Cayce believed, nothing happened out of nothing, and without reason. His unique metaphysical mind, tying in with the Universal Intelligence, had long ago told him of an order in the Universe with which man, cast in God's image (what He wanted us to be), was an integral part, given the free will to make a success or a failure of his life. To be a giver as well as a taker, a help to others, and not their oppressor. And even more to keep our minds open so we could grow with love of the Lord, not mock those who experienced His greatness—since it was all too apparent we couldn't live without the environment He had created for our development.

So with all humility and logic, Cayce was asked, why do we ignore the planets God created with the sun, the ruler, and the moon, the fair lady?

He replied: "He has given thee a mind, a body, an earth, and land in which to dwell. He has set the sun, the moon, the planets, the stars about thee to remind thee, even as the psalmist gave, 'Day unto day uttereth speech, night unto night showeth knowledge.' And yet how must the Savior feel when thee deny His day."

Cayce seemed to know more about the planets than our scientists whose quest for greater knowledge of the heavenly bodies was linked to the eternal mystery. He was asked, "Are any of the planets, in our solar system, other than the earth, inhabited by human beings or animal life of any kind?"

His answer: "No."

The first test, the moon. There were no greeting parties rushing to welcome our astronauts to their abode. The expedition to Mars was confined to a satellite rover, which had the planet pretty much to itself. Yet

Mars had as much energy and influence as any of the planets. And like the Moon, contributed to our language. The Moon, the inspiration of countless love songs, and Mars the symbol of military might. We looked at them so often they were like old friends.

Cayce rarely ducked a question on astrology. He was asked: "Do the planets have anything to do with the ruling of the destiny of man? If so, what? And what do they have to do with this body?"

"There is some connection," he replied. "In the beginning our own planet, Earth, was set in motion. The placing of the other planets began the ruling of the destiny of all matter as created, just as the division of the waters was and is ruled by the Moon in its path about the Earth. The strongest power in the destiny of man is the Sun, then the closer planets or those coming into ascendancy at the time of the birth of the individual. But let it be understood, no action of any planet or any of the phases of the Sun, Moon or any of the heavenly bodies surpass the rule of man's individual will, the power given by the Creator of man in the beginning when he became a living soul, and the faculty of choosing for himself."

I was intrigued by Cayce's interest in astrology. I make no case for astrology myself. Being neither for nor against it. Yet I have been impressed with some of the things astrologers can do, and with some of their clients who were not the kind of people to do anything off the beaten path unless they profited by it. In another generation, Evangeline Adams, the dean of astrologers and descendant of two American Presidents, bearing their name, counseled princes of finance like the elder J. P. Morgan, the railroad baron James J. Hill, and the newspaper magnate William Randolph Hearst on their financial matters.

Astrology intruded even in politics. In 1966, during a heated California gubernatorial campaign, Governor Edmund (Pat) Brown accused Republican Ronald Reagan of using astrology to beat him. Reagan, an Aquarian, merely smiled and kept blasting away as if victory was assured. And so it was. After his election, Governor Reagan was inaugurated at an unusual hour, just after midnight. But when astrology was mentioned, the former actor, and President-to-be, merely smiled. Years later, when he was President, the newspapers tried to make a scandal of a President—and a First Lady—using astrology. Nobody seemed to get stirred up but Reagan's political adversaries. The voters were too busy having their charts done by the neighboring astrologer.

Cayce may have been aware of it because he seemed to be aware of everything—that large corporations, as well as individuals, have made considerable use of astrology. Though some call it astrophysics, astrodynamics, astral cycles. RCA Communications, concerned about its shortwave radio messages, employed technician John Nelson to plot charts anticipating disruptive magnetic storms. They wouldn't call it astrology, though Nelson's storm warnings all hinged on the influence of the planets.

An electrical marvel, David Williams, cable purchasing manager of the New York utility, Consolidated

Edison, turned astrologer to anticipate periodic power slumps, attributed to changing planetary aspects—and bought miles of costly cable at depressed prices, while unwitting superiors wondered at his business acumen.

Williams not only plotted the price trends of commodities and the stock market, but did birth charts for many companies. For Philip Morris he correctly predicted a stock rise in a falling market in early 1970, and similarly advised officials of the New York telephone company they would get a rate increase they had applied for.

"The telephone company," Williams observed, "was a Gemini, born on June 18, and it was ruled by Mercury, the planet of communication. How could it miss?"

Even the rising popularity of astrology itself was attributed to the planets. For when Uranus, the symbol of the Aquarian Age and of astrology, in 1966 conjoined the planet Pluto, signifying the masses, in Virgo, the sign of service, astrology began its meteoric rise, staging a spectacular comeback after being associated for centuries with the Dark Ages.

The Ancients, the Greeks and the Romans, used astrology, ascribing various characteristics to the planets, which told me more where the Ancients were coming from than it did the planets. Cayce noted the influence of early mythology. Venus symbolizing love and beauty, which none can deny. Jupiter—Ennobling force, high ideals, good fortune, breadth of vision. Neptune—Mysticism, water, illusion. Uranus—Occult, drastic changes, extremes. Mercury—Mind, communications. Mars—

Anger, strife, high energy. Saturn—Stabilizing, limiting, teaching. Earth—Materialism, with accompanying emotions. The Sun—The source of light and life. The Moon—Feminine influences, intuition, romance, fluids, harmony in social relations.

Cayce had his reservations about astrology, deeming it paramount that man's free will dominate his life: "The vibrations from the various planets may at times seem harmful rather than helpful. The completeness and well-roundedness of the necessary experiences are important. For balance in this physical life is but a reflection of the necessary development in the spiritual life. The nobleness of Jupiter without the force of Mars; the love of Venus, without the tempering of Mercury, can be dangerous."

Man should call on his own inner reserves, he said, to resolve his problems: "There lies within him the ability, the power to choose that which signifies a step forward along the path. If one will make an effort, the knowledge of how to use to spiritual advantage any and all conditions will be opened from within. We become blinded by the needs we constantly magnify. Fear clutches our heart at the least sign of failure, and through lack of faith we lose our inner resolve."

One man he was advising had not been to a psychic before. He had consulted an astrologer, and mentioned this to Cayce before the reading. He was a successful businessman. Like many men who did well with their careers, he had problems with a marriage he had neglected because of his preoccupation with his business.

It was a story Cayce heard often. "Ye know," he

said, "this is something ye must settle within thyself. For only ye can make the decision in thine own heart which is more important to you."

"I have my children to think of," the man said. "I have to give them an education and launch their lives. I have to provide for them. I brought them on this earth."

"It was the Lord who gave them life," rejoined Cayce. "Never forget the Creator of all. And what decision you make with your marriage you make with His help. You alone, from within, you are responsible. The choice is yours. For the Lord gave you free will."

The man mused a moment. "I have made my own decisions all my life. I chose the wife I wed, now the mother of my children. I chose my profession. I chose the home we live in, and chose the career that made it possible. I have always considered my decisions before I make them. Usually listening to the recommendations of people I respect." He paused. "In this way I chose an astrologer. And"—he smiled—"in the same manner I chose you. The choice was mine, as you say. You see, I wanted a second opinion."

The Sleeping Prophet's lips seemed to part with a smile. His sense of humor never far from the surface. "And ye have been disappointed?"

"Not at all," said the businessman. "By and large you were both in agreement. I need to spend more time with my wife and children."

"Your own heart may have told you this had you considered from whence they came. Remember, the

Lord gave ye free will. Ye are the master of what you think and do. Always remember this. I am through."

With his Universal Mind, Cayce postulated the merits and demerits of astrology. "Astronomy is considered a science," he said, "and astrology a foolishness. One holds that because of the position of the earth, the sun and the planets are balanced one with another in some manner. Yet that they have nothing to do with man's life or the expanse of life, or the emotions of the physical body being in the earth.

"Then why and how do the effects of the Sun so influence other life on the earth and not affect man's life, man's emotions? As the sun has been set as the ruler of this solar system does it not appear to be reasonable that it has an effect upon the inhabitants of the earth as well as upon plant and mineral life in the earth? Then, if not, why? How then did the Ancients worship the sun as the representative of a continuous benevolent and beneficent influence upon the life of the individual?

"For remember, they—the sun, the moon, the planets—have their marching orders from the divine and they move in same. Man alone is given that birthright of free will. He alone may defy his God. But only so far. How many of you have questioned your own heart, and know that the disobedience in the earth reflects unto the heavenly hosts and thus influence that activity of God's command. For you—as sons and daughters of God—defy the living God too long. All the heavenly stars, the sun, are one in the various stages of consciousness or of activity for what? Man—Godly man. Yet when these become in defiance to that light which was commanded to march, to show forth the Lord's glory, His beauty, His mercy, His hope—His patience—do ye wonder then that there become reflected upon the face of the sun those turmoils and strifes that are the sin of man. All that was made to show to the sons, the souls, that God is mindful of His children."

I had done several books on Cayce, coining the phrase the Sleeping Prophet, yet I have never heard or seen anything of his counsel that appeared to be as thorough as this concern for the welfare of his fellow man. It is almost as though he was measuring the turmoil in nature against the behavior in man. And found man wanting. And so, as he did occasionally, he suggested that people take careful note of their everyday behavior. For the offense didn't have to be heinous or inhuman for the Lord to be displeased if it was an affront to the humble.

"How does a cross word affect thee? How does anger, jealousy, hate, animosity, affect thee as a son of God? If thou art the father of same, oft ye cherish the same. If thou art the recipient of same from others, thy brethren, how does it affect thee? Much as that confusion which is caused upon the earth by that which appears as the sun spot. The disruption of communications between men is what? These then become the influences that would show a man his littleness in entertaining hate, injustice or the lie.

"Be honest with thyself as thee would even ask the ruler of thy earth—the sun—to hearken to the voice of that which created it and to give its light irrespective of how ye act. For, as given, the sun shineth upon the just and the unjust alike. Yet it is often reflected in what happens to thee in thy journey through same."

Was Cayce being carried away by his concern for the good in the world that might be dissipated by those who ran roughshod over the Law of One that had been fatal to Atlantis?

"The more thee become aware of thy relationships to the universe and those influences that control same, the greater thy ability to rely upon the God force within. But still greater the responsibility to thy fellow man. For as thee do it to the least thee do it unto thy Maker. Even as to the sun which reflects those turmoils that arise with thee. Even as the earthquake, even as the wars and hates, even as the influences in thy life day by day.

"Then what are the sun spots? A natural consequence of the turmoil which the sons of God in the earth reflect upon the same. Let not thy hearts be troubled, yet believe in God. Then just act like it—to others.

"Hast thee created hope in thy association with thy fellow man? Yet ye fear and cringe when thee find that the spots upon thy sun cause confusion of any nature."

He felt the inclinations of man were ruled by the planets under which he was born. "In this the destiny of man lies within the sphere or scope of the planets. With the given position of the solar system at the time of the birth of an individual, it can be determined. That is, the inclinations and the actions—without the will power taken into consideration."

I thought of the businessman who had exercised free will in going to an astrologer and later consulting Cayce. Obviously, he could take the advice or leave it. More free will. Cayce had spoken of people consulting the stars long before anyone knew of the cosmic influence on our behavior. For instance, with a full moon, many surgeons postpone an operation for fear of excess bleeding because of the moon's effect on body fluid.

Cayce thought of astrology as a tool, as something that might be helpful to the individual.

He was frequently asked, "In what way should astrology be used to help man live better in the present physical plane?"

He responded as he would to a similar question about the Millennium, for he felt the individual reflected an inner uncertainty about what the event would bring:

"Since the positions of the planets give the tendencies in a given life, then let man, the individual, understand how his will may be altered in any situation. With that God force manifested in the creation of man, dictating the choice between good and evil.

"Destiny then," Cayce went on, "is indeed in the hands of the individual. For He, the Lord, hath given. 'Though ye be far, if ye call I will hear.' If ye be unto thy brethren, unto thy associates, unto those about thee as a channel of blessings, then He thy Father, thy God, will direct thee in the ways thou should go. Learn ye then, to know Him as thine own Father, to whom ye may go in joy and in sorrow. In whatever may be thy experience let thy light, thyself, so shine before thy fellow man that others may know that ye walk oft with Him."

In speaking of the Millennium years before its arrival, Cayce saw the era off to a good start because of the New Age planet Uranus in the New Age sign of Aquarius. "Uranus brings out those of the spiritual side of life, especially of the motive forces." He thought of Uranus as an active force. It dealt with an area he had been connected with all his life. "In Uranus the activity makes for an interest in those things of the occult or the mystical nature. And these bring the entity oft those things that are most helpful."

Elsewhere he said of the Uranus-Aquarians, the star children of the Millennium: "For the Lord hath not willed that any soul should perish. Thus he gives thee the opportunities to glory in thy association with the living God."

And that was most fortuitous, for the outset of the Millennium at any rate. He was optimistic: "Ye are today what ye are because of what ye were on the yesterday. And what ye are today is the shadow of that which will be thy experience on what ye call the morrow."

And there would be many tomorrows.

Cayce's promise. This is what he saw, with the in-

Chapter Thirteen
A Message for the Millennium

"You young men shall dream dreams, your old men shall see visions, your maidens shall prophesy."

Edgar Cayce was very comfortable with what he saw for the Millennium. It would be a new world, with some of the old ways of prejudice and ego holding up things for a while, but it would be a world which the Lord would approve. There would be earthquakes in places where the earth was settling itself in a normal way, but as a new brotherhood began to emerge, nations would try to help rather than hinder each other—unlikely as this might seem as one ponders the current state of affairs around the world. But harmony would come as we got into the Millennium. This was Edgar Cayce's promise. This is what he saw, with the return—with His Presence—of the One who so often walked alone, and the benign influence of a Universal God whose realm extended to the most distant planets and solar systems. For, as Cayce saw, He was not only the Creator but Creation itself, alive in all of us if we would only open our hearts.

For centuries the prophets of doom had looked to the striking of the New Age as a time of woe, comparable to the eclipse of storied Atlantis, which they saw as a precedent for the downfall of a civilization unable to contain the savage wars and massacres that have marked its history since Adam and Eve ate the apple.

However, Edgar Cayce, the greatest mystic and prophet of our time, shrugged, and with a little smile took off his shoes and laid down on a couch, listening to people who were coming to him with concerns over not only their fate, but the fate of their children and grandchildren.

He had said time after time that none of the cataclysms and associated horrors would have to occur if man would only listen to the simple commandments coming from Sinai and the lips of Christ and others like Buddha, wise beyond *his* times:

"The New Age is as near or as distant as we make it. But will surely come with the Millennium. We must prepare ourselves to meet the Redeemer as a bride prepares herself to meet her husband, by being pure, lovable, selfless, self-sacrificing. We cannot enjoy the perfect unless we ourselves are perfect.

"Is the New Age spiritual or physical? Both. We have first to spiritualize the physical before we can take it with us into spiritual realms. That is what Christ did. He is still the Way.

"The New Age will be no experiment, but a reality, a truth." As Cayce did so often, he then quoted from the Bible, a book he recommended that everybody read. " 'In that day,' the prophet Hosea said of the Lord, 'I will make a covenant for them with the beasts of the field and with the fowls of the heaven and with the creeping things of the ground, and I will break the bow and the sword and the battle out of the earth, and will make them to lie down safely.

" 'The great will be at peace with the humble. The weak ones in Christ will be strong. It is now dawn for those who will make themselves ready for the New Age. And the Fisherman sayeth unto me, Seal not the sayings of the prophecy of this book. For the time is at hand. He that is unjust, let him be unjust still. He that is filthy, let him be filthy still. He that is righteous, let him be righteous still. And he that is holy, let him be holy still.'

"For the law of the Lord is love, and it is in each soul that it finds the answer to those promises as He hath made. Those promises are for each soul. For He is the church, the bridegroom for each soul that seeks to know his face, and His ways. And He is not slack, as men, in keeping those promises to those who are faithful in seeking the Spirit of Truth. For as He hath given, 'As ye do it unto the least of my children, ye do it unto me.'

"Let not thy heart be troubled, neither be afraid. For as ye seek, as ye live, so will it be measured unto thee and thine. For the love of the Father casteth out fear, and brings that assurance of His abiding presence with thee. So surround thyself by thought, by deed, by act, with the consciousness of the Christ that no man, no group, no thought can hurt thee.

"Thy future life is in thine own making. For know He, the Father, hath made thee a free-willed individual. So choose ye whom ye will serve. There is set before thee life and death, good and evil. As to what, as to which, as to where, as to how ye will choose, this is within thine own consciousness. Choose thou, and let thy prayer ever be: 'Oh, Lord, Maker of heaven and earth, Giver of life and love, be thou near unto me. Make me a channel, oh God, of blessings to others day by day.'

"There is in the vision of the New Age the new understanding, the new seeking for the relationships of a Creative Force to the sons of men. Then as ye show forth the fruits of the spirit, then, indeed, the purposes are to manifest in such measures that they who are weak take hope. They who have faltered gain new courage. They who are disappointed and disheartened gain a new concept of hope that springs eternally within the human breast.

"Remember above all, as He hath given, 'As ye do it unto the least of thy brethren, of thy associates, of thy companions, day by day, ye do it unto thy God.' Yea, the God within thyself. For God is not mocked, and He knows what is in thine heart."

Cayce had reached deep inside himself, concerned about his country and other countries, which he saw consumed by a self-interest and lack of caring that was opposed to everything God had planned for the creature—man—he gave free will with the intent of his proving himself.

As the Millennium drew closer in the Twentieth Century, the rumbling of the earth was unabated, and an uneasiness grew among the people who beat a path to the prophet's door.

Some were disturbed by a book saying very ominously, referring to America: "There shall be few where there were many. Tens replacing thousands. It is written that after a thousand years, Satan shall be loose for a season. This is well, for the race possessing such amazing powers, though few will be the people."

Many were reassured by Cayce's response. He said they could rely on the Lord in the name of the Lamb of God. So there was always a choice. And that choice extended to the End Times and the Millennium. And the Lord. "Be sure," said Cayce, "that you are among those that chose."

In the same vein, he was asked, with increasing concern as time wore on: "What is meant by 'The day of the Lord is near at hand'?"

"That as has been promised, through the prophets and sages of old, the time and half times has been and is being fulfilled in this day and generation. And that soon, when there will again appear in the Earth that One through whom many will be called to meet those that are preparing the way for His day in the Earth. He, then, will come, even as ye have seen Him go."

And when would this happen?

"When those that are His have made the way clear and passable for Him to come."

Although the questions pouring out of people revealed only self-concern, Cayce was always encouraging, seeing the rainbow in the darkest cloud:

"So let us be up and doing, for the night cometh, when no man can work. But this does not mean death. It does not mean the close of day."

Much of what Cayce was saying was hardly new. Some of it was in the Bible, his lifelong companion, but he would take it and go, applying it to the present day, and what he saw ahead. One thousand years of peace, after a fairly rough beginning. He saw a fresh start, with new leaders dedicated to bringing people together, not stressing their own political advantage.

He recommended that the nation's leaders turn more to the Bible and less to the front pages, as they grappled with what was best for all the people. Without subservience to any cult or religion, but through fairness and common sense. He always made the point there was only one God—not your God, nor my God, but everyone's God. For all of creation is the same to the Creator. We are all part of the same puzzle, with God having the answers.

"So know that your prayers are not cast on empty sands and seas," Cayce said. "All knowledge that ye may have is within self. For thy body, thy mind, thy soul, is part of God's universal consciousness. But know the application of same is not to the glory of self but to Him who is the truth and the light."

People wanted to know how they could write a better book, build a stronger bridge, have a happier marriage, or make more money. He would answer the questions, correct the lack in their lives, then stress that all this would be meaningless if they didn't choose the Universe Club over the elitist University Club.

Time and again, he was asked how this world of his had begun and when it would end, as distinguished from the world of the spirit that he invariably talked about at great length.

His reply: The world at large is still being created. The process is virtually endless. Another way of saying there would be no foreseeable end. For this planet was created in the image of the Creator. As Cayce saw, the Creator and Creation were commingled. As the great scientist Einstein said, dwelling on the unfathomable universe, there is no time or space, but a continuing force given life by the will of God given to man.

"With the evolving of man," Cayce said, "God gave man the soul and mind that he might make himself one with Creation. Without application to the animal kingdom. Look at history. Which has survived? The brute strength or the development toward that of God? Which survives—the man that embraces God and seeks to emulate His forces and powers, or the man that emulates the forces of evil and flesh? This answers itself. For as it all began in the mind of the Creator, there came the point, the place, the beginning when that as created was done. Creation is always evolving. The earth's sphere, the first misty Creation in the mind of the Creator, has the same Creative Energy. For God is the same yesterday, today and forever. And the same in one Creation creates that same in another Creation. With man given then the will and the soul to make itself One with Creation. Through being the beneficiary of the Creative Energy and God. With man surviving disasters in the plant and animal kingdoms, as geological surveys show, he thus became the only survivor of that original Creation. On through this Millennium and others."

Cayce's saga appeared to be a provocative compromise between the scientific concept of evolution and the biblical Garden of Eden, with the latter tying humanity closer to God.

In the main, Cayce was concerned with the impact of events on those who were the heart and soul of any country. The future, he believed, belonged to them, extraordinary ordinary man.

"Destiny is in the hands of the individual, for He hath given, 'Though ye be far, if ye call I will hear.' If ye be unto thy brethren, unto those about thee, as a channel of blessings, then He thy Father, thy God, will direct thee in the ways ye should go."

Cayce's own belief system was so strong that it conveyed his trust in God to the people he counseled. It was a personal God he saw, not remote, interested in each and everyone, as the Head of a house, caring for His children:

"Learn ye then to know him as thine own Father, to whom ye may go in joy, in sorrow, in distress. In whatever may be thy experience let thy light, thy self, so shine before thy fellow man that others may know that ye walk with Him. He that climbeth up some other way deceives himself and gives credit where none is due."

What Cayce was obviously saying was if the individual went outside himself in a materialistic way, he gained nothing within himself of the spirit.

"Always remember the Lord thy God is one. The activities of thy body, thy mind, thy soul should then be as one. Each experience to thy self makes for regeneration, uplift, which become the means for bringing harmony and peace to the inner self."

Nothing Cayce did had more importance than getting people on the path to God. For then, as he saw, with the increase in God-mindedness, if not Godliness, a new world could be born with the New Age that would bring a higher consciousness to millions. It had to begin somewhere, and where better than in the minds of those looking for some serenity in their lives?

"Turn within and not without when thy disturbances arise, and know that He hath promised to meet thee in thy temple. As the body is the temple of the soul. And there He hath promised to meet thee. His promises are sure if ye but allow thyself to draw upon them in joy as in sorrow. In the ups and the downs. For thy God is not a God of wrath, nor of hate, but a God of love. And not only in thine distresses praise Him, thank Him, but be consistent in thine experiences, in thine seeking. For the natural tendency is to go to extremes when one is very much elated over that which is bubbling over. For a kindness, a gentleness to a fellow person brings more harmony into self than some great deed that may be well spoken of. For this is soon forgotten, but the fruits of the spirit—as be experienced in thy daily life—becomes wells of living water, springing up within thy self to bring that joy that comes from knowing Him."

As the years passed, Cayce became involved with the thought that only the Creator could save His Creation. Of which man was not the least. For had He not created man in His divine image? Not that he should be a divinity, but think and act divinely. For man, with his integrity and closeness to his Maker, was given the Promised Land. If there was love in God's world, and only hate elsewhere, with one war after another, one injustice heaped on others, how much longer could a troubled world carry the burden without breaking up, as that other world had so long ago?

Yes, and there was a better world for those who pleased the Lord. For in this universe of many solar systems there were many places where man's heart and soul might fulfill the desire for a haven where his spirit could express its yearnings for a life separated from the eternal loneliness of man.

"Man," said Cayce, again out of his Bible, "may not live by bread alone. Nor by gratifying of appetites in the material world. For man is not made for this world alone. There is a longing for those experiences belonging to the soul. For without spirituality the earth may indeed be a hell. However, since the body is the temple of the living God, act like it. Keep it clean. Don't desecrate it. Keep it such that it may be the place where thou may meet thine own better self, thine own God-self. As ye do this there may be harmony, peace, joy. As in everything if ye would have joy ye must give others joy. If ye would have love, ye must love. If ye would have friends, be friendly. And with patience, ye will find such within.

"Keep thy heart, thy mind, thy purposes, attuned to that voice within, knowing where there is thy altar. There He has promised to meet thee. Be mindful of the service, of the assurance, of the manner of the offering ye make there to Him. That is how and why, as He has given, 'As the man thinketh in his heart so is he.'

"Work then to show thyself approved unto God, stressing each phase of thy life. Not only of spirit, nor mind, nor matter, but each consistent with the other, that ye present thy body, holy and acceptable as a gift unto Him who hath need of love, even as thou hast need of love."

This was a thought I had not heard elsewhere: that the omnipotent Lord of all Creation needed love just as we, His ungrateful children, do.

"As we wait on the Lord," said Cayce, "we establish this close relationship of Father and Son. When the Son—as thee—is worthy of the love of an all-wise Father. Everything is possible for the Father, and no good will be withheld from the Son. Sadly, it remains to be seen what one can accomplish, who chooses to give himself wholly over to the will of the Father.

"It was said that we not judge lest we be judged. Before we question the actions of a brother, let us first seek the motive that prompted the act. It would make us more fit to sit in judgment, if we dared to do so. Do we know the cause that prompted a crime, or even the thought that preceded it? Do we know the cause for the flower to bloom or the grass to be green? Since we ourselves know so little, how can we judge the activities of another?

"Let us remember that love is God and that unselfish love and judgments spring from Him. No matter where it is manifested. It is not only a privilege, but His command, that we love one another.

"Do not hesitate to do what thy conscience tells thee is right. Each moment we live is the only time. We cannot wait. For in the waiting we weaken our will and lose opportunities. The field is ready. Never before have we had a greater opportunity. Never were there so many in high places ready to help or be helped. Is it we who falter or the powers that be holding us back? Are we afraid for self that we do not rush to righteousness in greater service, more prayer, more meditation, more healing and thanksgiving?

"We need now as always men—leaders—unafraid. Socrates [the Greek philosopher] who drank the hemlock for truth's sake, not fearing death. Christian martyrs who chose the flames of torture, for their love of Christ. For what do we stand? What is our purpose, our ideal in these trying times? We must do all we can."

In the final sequence of his life, his own Millennium, as he put it, the great prophet of our times saw the relationship of man to his Creator as more tangible and consequential than any El Niño or eruption of the earth.

As he lapsed into the biblical idiom, Cayce conveyed a broader meaning of greater intensity, far more personal to man's relationship to his Maker:

"In His close union between God the Father and His children, He has hidden nothing from them. They are warned of dangers, comforted in sorrows. In the light and understanding of God, we as His children may realize His love for man. It is too wonderful for many to fully comprehend, for man is so often blinded by greed, self-indulgence and hate. He has shut the door to wisdom which only love can open. We cannot serve two Masters. It is either we serve God through serving others, or serve where self alone is benefited.

"It is a union that depends on man's virtue, even as the New Age arrives, for the Lord is not fickle. His desire for man's love constant."

The Holy Spirit manifesting today is Christ's promise fulfilled. As John the Beloved said, "And I [Jesus] will pray to the Father and He shall give you another Comforter that He may abide with you forever, even as the spirit of truth." A spirit that Cayce saw as God in action. His coming may be as a mighty wind or as a gentle murmur, but to the soul who is seeking, He is known by his benevolence. There is no greater ecstasy we can experience than the realization we are counted worthy of this heavenly visitor and the promise of His eternal presence among us. Father, Son and Holy Spirit—these are One.

Cayce saw the intermittent wars of a war-weary world bringing a desperate need for hope and solace as so many turned to the Lord when they had no other place to turn:

"So often soldiers have expressed how they have felt the protective power of God while in action. Officers have been converted in strange ways. With one it came about while carrying out his duties censoring the mails. Many of the letters written to parents and wives expressed great faith and showed their religion had become a living thing as they became more spiritual. With the spiritual forces. To know the world outside one must first know the world within. Of the earth is the physical man made. But of the Universe is the mind and infinite soul. Thus the study of self comes first and foremost in him that would be a good neighbor and friend. That would be the greater experience, the ability to serve those cast in the image of the Maker. For as ye do it unto the least of thy brethren ye do it unto God."

It remained for a sleeping Cayce to define the closeness of the Lord. As we did our share. "Let us seek to become aware of God and our near relationship with Him. Be aware of the blessings, the opportunities He has put in our way. Opportunities which show us that God is mindful of us. We are wise if we embrace them, not for self-glory, but for the glory of our Maker. The first awareness of each soul should be a recognition of God's love for him."

As Cayce recalled from the apostle Peter, "If we would become aware of how much difference there would be in our choice made day by day, knowing how mindful He is of us, that He has not willed that any soul should perish."

Cayce had the feeling the upcoming Millennium

would be very special, if only because of man's discovery of the God within. At the same time realizing in a way almost physical that the Lord was aware of everyone of us:

"How could He who created the planets and solar systems so many times greater than our earth, who numbered a woman for each man, so that all could mate—how could He not know what goes on inside every one of us?

"God knows each life in the same manner as it is manifested in a grain of wheat. What a union there is between the Father and His children. They are warned of dangers and comforted in sorrows. In Him all law is observed.

"And if it comes to violence, what then? How does the Lord feel about the weaponry man has fashioned, as in long ago Atlantis? Enough to extinguish himself from His Earth, as was done in another place. Is it like the match play of children about to be burned? Will it be soon before He intervenes? Only He knows. But when He decides His ire will be sure and swift. For He cannot allow His children to again destroy what He built with loving care. But they know the signs, and the history of the past. That they toy with forces beyond their control. And they will listen.

"As He decides, He will strike like the lightning. For this He will send the Savior, the Son, as the final measure to impose a peace without the eruptions of ancient Atlantis, which destroyed the many nations. The Son will give the Word. The skies will darken, the mountains tremble, and the oceans dry up. But none will die. For the Word was love. The Lord had pronounced many generations of peace, where man could count His blessings and seek out the Son who gave the Word for the Father. And the Word was still love. And this time the people listened. For they had seen the Son heal the sick, part the waves, and raise the dead."

Would the Word be sufficient? Cayce thought so:

"As never before man is being called to stand forth and be counted on the side of creativity or destruction. The average person does not realize that choices made daily, by the moment, are part of this responsibility to choose this day whom you will serve.

"It is the will, a divine heritage, which must be exercised daily. The pattern of the mind may be destructive. The will must oppose this pattern and hold to ideals and purposes. In times of war men are trained for fighting. Fear and hate are magnified until it becomes natural to think, speak and act destructively. Only a strong will can turn a life from such a path. Even when the war has ceased men will continue to enjoy the excitement of argument, contention, fear and hate in their lives. Only careful self-observation, the weighing of positives and negatives in the smallest decisions will bring needed balance. Through man recognizing himself as co-creator with God can man grasp the importance of his choice."

Cayce was optimistic, more for the future than the present. "This America of ours, hardly a new Atlantis, will have another thousand years of peace, another Millennium. All this done in the same manner that the prayers of ten just men once saved a city. And then the deeds, the prayers of the faithful will glorify the Father as peace and love will reign for those who love the Lord. Amen."

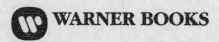